Skating in the Arts of 17th Century Holland

by Laurinda S. Dixon

*An exhibition honoring the
1987 World Figure Skating Championships*

The Taft Museum
Cincinnati, Ohio

March 5-April 19, 1987

Introduction and Acknowledgements

No sooner had our local newspapers begun to announce that Cincinnati would host the 1987 World Figure Skating Championships than the concept for this exhibition was born. The Taft Museum, so richly endowed with 17th century Dutch landscapes, portraits, and genre paintings, is ideally suited to organize the first comprehensive survey of ice skating as an artistic subject. *Skating in the Arts of 17th Century Holland* exemplifies the type of exhibition in which we take the greatest pride, for it educates and entertains, uniting our museum with its downtown audience of residents and visitors.

We have been most fortunate to secure the participation of Dr. Laurinda S. Dixon as our guest curator. Her published studies on the arts of the Northern Renaissance are broadly conceived and meticulously researched. As a member of the art history faculty at Syracuse University, she continues to refine a multi-disciplinary approach in her lectures that wins her teaching accolades. Her knowledge and enthusiasm for art and life are conspicuous in the works she has chosen for this exhibit and in the essay she has authored for this catalogue. From her work we learn to understand artistic developments in the context of human experience. Figure skating emerges as a pastime, as a sport, and also a metaphor of social conduct with both moral and political meanings. One who has seen this show and read its message will certainly approach the local ice rink in a new frame of mind.

In her acknowledgments Dr. Dixon thanks the many individuals who have assisted her in the organization of this exhibition. I would like to add my thanks to hers, for as always such ambitious projects can only be realized when colleagues share our inspirations and give generously of their time and expertise. I would also like to join Laurinda in praising the many talents of our registrar David Torbet Johnson, who coordinated the exhibition through all its phases.

The lenders to this exhibition have done us the great honor of endorsing our vision by entrusting us with their matchless treasures. On behalf of all who will see *Skating in the Arts of 17th Century Holland,* may I offer to these collectors and institutions the sincerest thanks of the Taft Museum.

Ruth K. Meyer
Director

LENDERS TO THE EXHIBITION:

Butler Library, Rare Book and Manuscript Library, Columbia University, New York, NY
Mr. Dick Button
Cincinnati Art Museum, Cincinnati, OH
The Folger Shakespeare Library, Washington, DC
High Museum of Art, Atlanta, GA
Hood Museum of Art, Dartmouth College, Hanover, NH
The Library of Congress, Washington, DC
Frederick and Jan Mayer
The Metropolitan Museum of Art, New York, NY
Museum of Fine Arts, Boston, MA
The Newberry Library, Chicago, IL
The New York Public Library, New York, NY
The National Gallery of Art, Washington, DC
The Pierpont Morgan Library, New York, NY
Princeton University Library, Princeton, NJ
United States Figure Skating Association, World Figure Skating Hall of Fame and Museum, Colorado Springs, CO

In arranging an exhibition with lenders from many
locations, while at the same time gathering material for
an accompanying catalogue, one incurs a great many
debts which can never be repaid with a simple verbal
acknowledgement. Nevertheless, to those who have
aided me with their generosity and countless courtesies,
I offer you my thanks. I begin by thanking Ruth
Meyer, director of the Taft Museum, who conceived the
idea for this exhibition, for her encouragement and
guidance from the original planning stages exhibition to
the final installation. I also thank David Johnson,
registrar for the Taft Museum, for easing the trauma of
my absentee curatorship by shouldering several of the
curatorial responsibilities required to bring this
exhibition into being.

In addition, I wish to thank the curatorial and
library staffs at the following institutions for their
personal assistance: The Library of Congress,
Washington, DC; the Folger Shakespeare Library,
Washington, DC; The Metropolitan Museum of Art,
New York City; The York Public Library, New York
City; and the Museum of Fine Arts, Boston. Robin
Adèr, curator of prints at the Museum Boymans-van
Beuningen, Rotterdam, must also be thanked for his
energetic efforts on behalf of the exhibition, though
limitations in funding did not allow borrowing from
foreign sources.

Recognition must go to a few extraordinary
individuals, without whom this exhibition would have
been less than it is. For adding their wisdom to the
writing of the catalogue, I thank Johanna Prins, who
gave poetic beauty to her Dutch translations, and
Donald Mills, who lent his scholarly expertise to
translating passages in Latin. Acknowledgement also
goes to David Broda for his photographic expertise
and Chuck Klaus for his editorial assistance. Special
gratitude goes to Dick Button, for opening his vast
private collection of skating art to the Taft Museum,
and to Helen Cataldi, curator of the collections of the
United States Figure Skating Museum in Colorado
Springs, for her boundless energy and kind solicitude
on my behalf. I also thank Benjamin T. Wright,
chairman of the World Figure Skating Museum, for
generously approving the large number of loans from
his institution, without which this exhibition would not
have been possible. To all the museums, private
collectors and individuals who were involved in this
exhibition, I thank you for your contributions.

Laurinda S. Dixon

Skating in the Arts of 17th Century Holland

Though human history spans several thousands of years, ice skating is only documented visually from the 15th century onward and then almost exclusively in Northern art and most predominantly in the 17th century. The skating scene, at least one of which can be found in nearly every art museum in this country, is closely related to the unique social, economic and religious circumstances of the Low Countries during this time. In fact, ice skating as a subject for artists coincides with a time when the popularity of pictures devoted to other than religious subjects reached a peak. In part, this new secularization of art was caused by the Protestant distrust of Catholic religious images; however, the tastes of the wealthy Dutch merchant class for paintings in the home played a large part in the development of new subject matter.

By the 17th century, the Church had largely been displaced by the secular public as the major art patron. In response to this situation, artists freely devised alternative themes that reflected the hard-won "good life" that Dutch burghers prized. Painted still-life displays perpetuated the luxuriant sight of rich tables heaped with gastronomic delicacies served in expensive imported dishes. Landscapes that record the broad vistas and vast clouded skies of the Low Countries immortalized Dutch national pride. Genre paintings exalted scenes of daily life that were fraught with both humor and pain. The portrait tradition thrived as a vehicle for representing the industry, practicality and individual initiative of the merchant classes. By the 17th century, no comfortable home was lacking in pictures reflecting the new subject matter. Skating scenes, which often combined the categories of landscape and genre subjects, were widely sought by the 17th-century public.[1]

Dutch art collectors, in addition to being wealthy, were also literate. They liked their pictures full of content and meaning, purportedly to challenge their minds, but more likely to remove any suggestion of frivolity from their collecting. For this reason, Dutch art often conceals a deeper meaning beneath the surface. Allegory and symbolism were inherited from an earlier age, when complex systems of pictorial iconography served to explicate the mysteries of the Catholic Church. By the 17th century, thinking, speaking and painting in riddles had become a popular social pastime. For the Dutch, pictures of ice skating called forth an entire roster of hidden meanings couched in everyday forms.

Dutch skating scenes, by combining realism and allegory, reveal the 17th century as an era much like our own. Artistic genius records that Dutch folk of the 17th century were very much like Americans today— pragmatic and creative—patriotic and individualistic— hoping for the best, yet prepared for the worst. We see from these works, so innocent and engaging on the surface, that the frolicking skaters in fact represent a world view that was quite often despairing and pessimistic. Their world, like ours, was devastated by wars that, though contained, were global in nature. 17th century physicians, like modern ones, were dumfounded by the sudden emergence of incurable diseases never before documented in the history of medicine.[2]

On the other hand, there was much to be hopeful about. Exploration and discovery had greatly enlarged the boundaries of both the terrestrial and the celestial worlds, offering undreamed-of opportunities for intellectual expansion.[3] Concurrently, the authority of conservative Church dogma had been broken, allowing social and cultural experimentation unprecedented in the history of the world. Vast written evidence survives to document this exciting period in history; however, it is mute art that conveys the most eloquent remembrance of the "Golden Age" of Dutch culture. This exhibition explores the significance of ice skating in the context of 17th century Dutch art—from the first crude woodcut print in the 15th century (Cat. #34) to the sophisticated atmospheric paintings of Pieter Bruegel the Elder (Cat. #1), Aert van der Neer (Cat. #2) and Barent Avercamp (Cat. #3). In so doing, modern viewers can gain a deeper appreciation for a remarkable sport immortalized during a remarkable period in history.

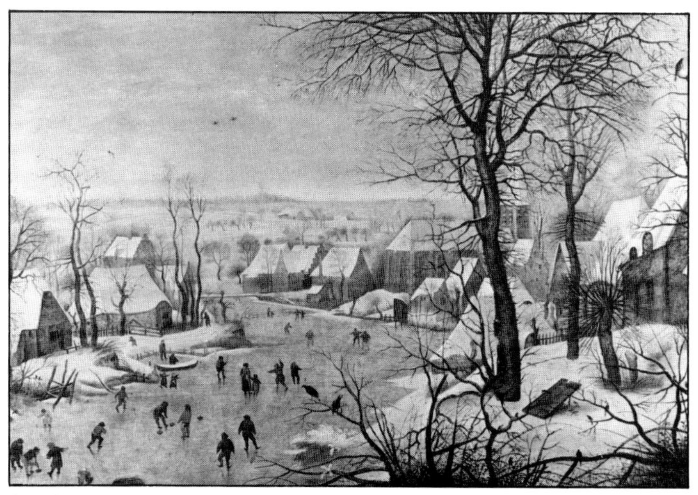

Cat. #1

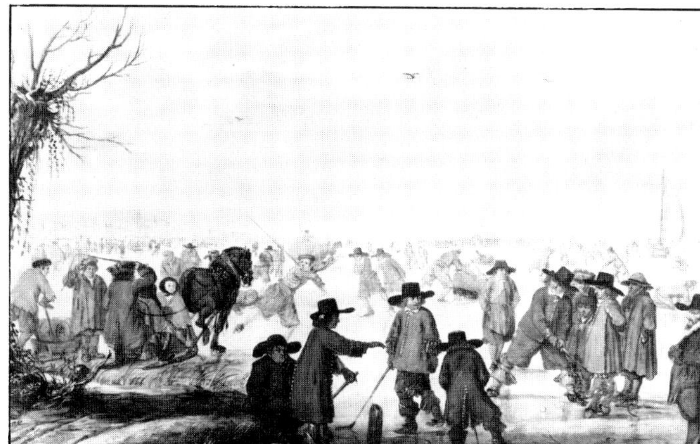

Cat. #3

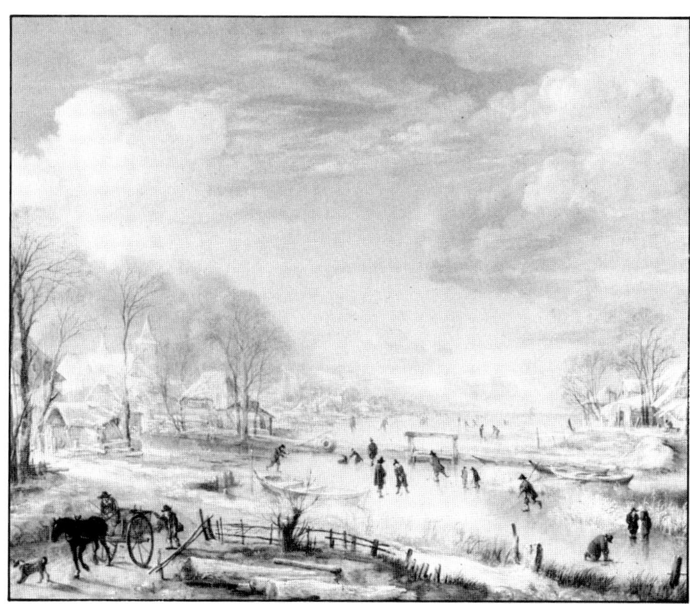

Cat. #2

The History Of Ice Skating

Ice skating appeared in the historical record long before it was depicted in art. The earliest depictions found in Scandinavian sagas and runic poetry imply that skating was among the eight or nine essential accomplishments of noble warriors.[4] Among the legends of the *skrid finnae*, or "sliding Finns," is a poem that boasts, "I know how to perform eight exercises: I fight with courage; I keep a firm seat on horseback; I am skilled in swimming; I glide along the ice on skates; I excel in darting the lance; I am dextrous with the oar; and yet a Russian maid disdains me!"[5] Oller, the ancient Scandinavian god of winter, was an expert skater, running over the ice at super-human speed on blades made from animal bones.[6] Archaeological evidence suggests that ice skating began in remote glacial areas of the world for the purposes of migration, hunting and waging war. The sport we love so well was born of necessity, not of pleasure.

Historians disagree about who introduced ice skating into Western Europe. Presumedly, the skill came to England from the Continent in 1066, along with William the Conqueror, the French language and a strange breed of practical beast called the "horse."[7] Whatever the case, twenty years later Thomas à Becket's secretary, a man known as "Fitzstephen," wrote a Latin *Discription of the Most Noble City of London* in which he noted "many young men playing on the ice…some tye bones to their feete and under their heeles, and shoving themselves with a little picked staffe do slide as swiftlie as a birde flyeth in the aire or an arrow out of a cross-bow."[8] Judging by Fitzstephen's wondering tone, hard frosts were infrequent in 12th-century Europe. How, then, did skating become the "national sport" of Holland?

In fact, natural ice was rare in the days before artificial refrigeration. Medieval Europe enjoyed a relatively temperate climate, much like it does today. Beginning in about 1400, however, the world's climate underwent a sudden change. For four hundred years, a short period of time in geological terms, Northern Europe was plunged into what has since been termed the *kleine ijstijd* or "little ice age" that is well documented in literature and art.[9] The first painter to make winter a special part of his art was Pieter Bruegel the Elder. His *Winter Landscape with Bird Trap* (Cat. #1) illustrates, by means of masterful monochromatic color scheme, skaters frolicking amid the chill of a winter day. Later, books like Reinzer's *Meteorologia philosophico-politica…*(Cat. #4) would illustrate the frozen fountains and bare branches of particularly harsh winters. Glacial cold embraced all of Europe—even the temperate lagoon of Venice froze solid (Cat. #5). In Holland, the web of inland canals that served cities for commercial transportation became ice-bound during a large part of the year, freezing boats where they lay in the water (Cat. #6). Today the waterways rarely freeze in Holland, and when they do, it is an occasion for national celebration. In the 16th century, however, the situation was devastating. Another people might have been defeated by the sudden crippling of their major means of trade and transportation. The resourceful Dutch, however, turned what could have been a national disaster into a unique advantage.

Skating became a way of life and a means for commercial advancement in the Low Countries. Dutch musketeers went to war on skates, just as the old Norsemen did in ancient times. According to accounts of the Battle of the River Ij fought in 1572 against the Spanish, Dutch troops wearing skates crossed the frozen river and took the enemy by surprise. The Spanish captain promptly ordered several thousand pairs of skates for his own soldiers. The Spaniards, however, lacked both the will and the skill to succeed, and the scheme failed.[10] Back home, women skated to market, and taverns pitched tents on the frozen canals. Here, the sale of hot milk, coffee, schnapps and warm wine was advertised by a wreath hung from the top of a horizontal pole in front of the tent (Cat. #13). Occasionally, a dice bucket was hung on the pole to advertise gambling, which was sometimes allowed on the ice but forbidden in the city.[11] Far from being reduced to frozen wastelands, canals became busy thoroughfares, utilized by all levels of Dutch society.

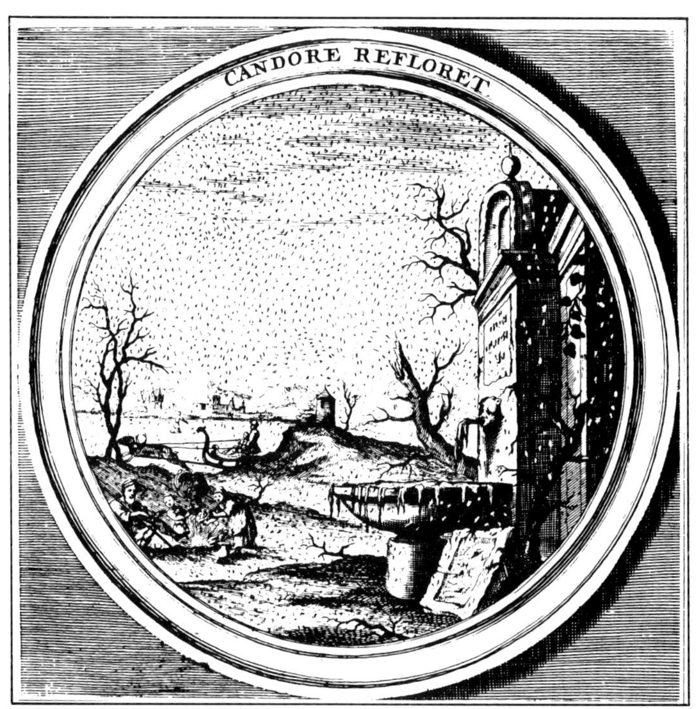

Cat. #4

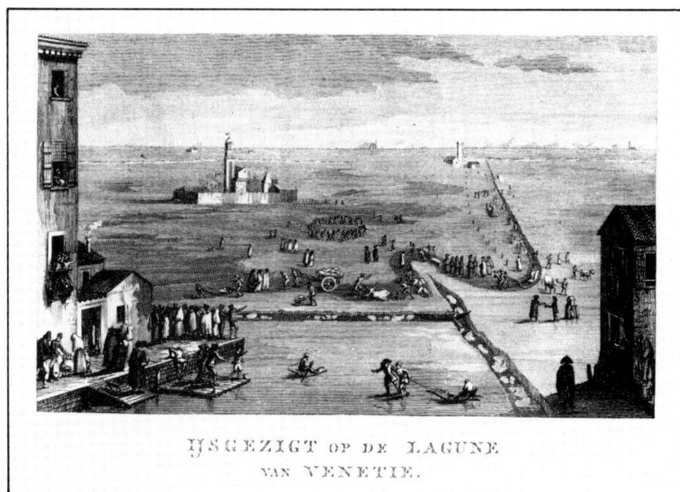

Cat. #5

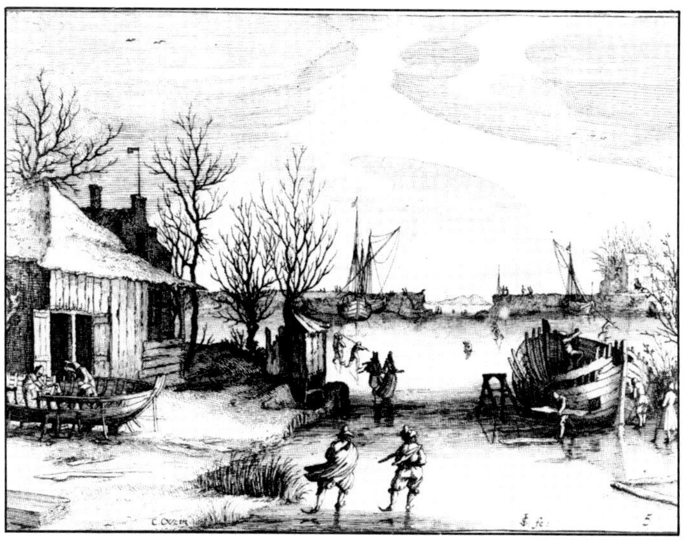

Cat. #6

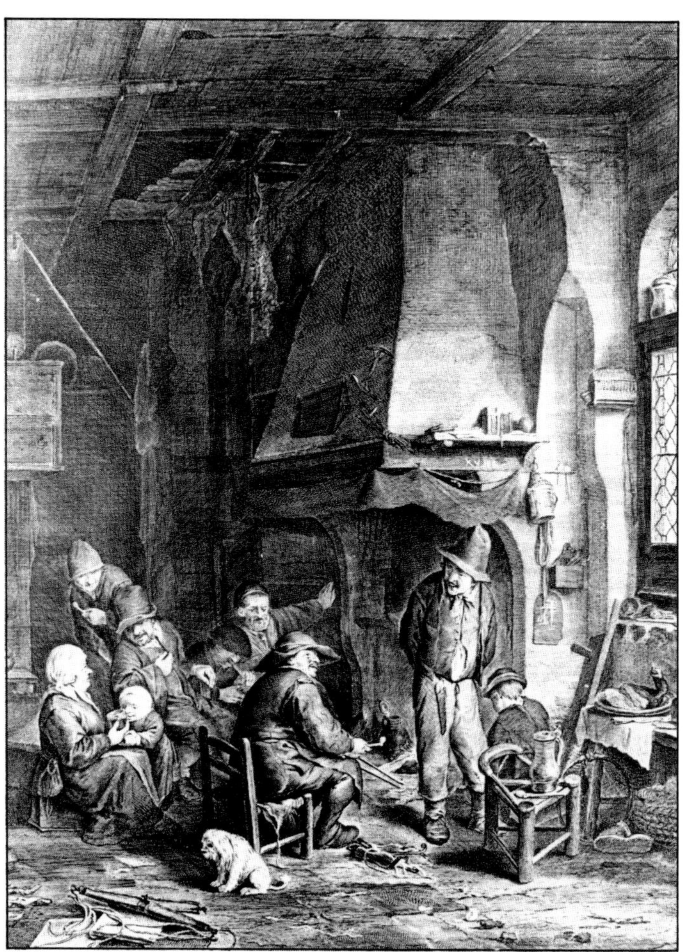

Cat. #7

THE EARLY ART OF ICE SKATING

The earliest skates—those that sped the old Norse god Oller across frozen water—were made of bone (Fig. 1). The oldest pair in existence today were found in a Swiss lake and are thought to date from about the year 3,000 B.C. Other prehistoric examples have surfaced in Scandinavia, Holland and England, attesting to the widespread practice of skating among our early ancestors. Archaeological evidence suggests that ancient skates were made from the metacarpal bone of a large animal, such as a horse, deer or sheep. Holes were bored in each end through which leather thongs were threaded to bind the skates to the feet. These prehistoric skates, so different from modern blades, were about a foot long, smooth and flat on the bottom, indicating that they may have evolved from skis or sled runners. It would have been difficult, on sliders like these, to negotiate backward or sideways movements. Primitive people probably pushed themselves along the ice with poles, much like cross-country skiers. Significantly, the word *schenkel*, meaning "shank" or "leg bone," is still used in Holland when describing a modern steel skate.[12]

Figure 1 Prehistoric bone skate (Colorado, USFSA)

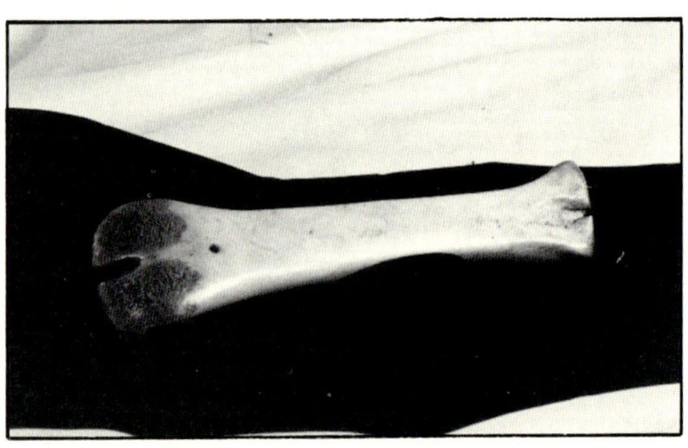

Iron skates were first mentioned in around 200 A.D. by the Swedish bishop Olaus Magnus (Oloff Mansson) in his *Historia de Gentium Septentrionalium*...(Cat. #8). This book, which existed in handwritten manuscript form long before it was first published in 1555, contains woodcuts illustrating every possible activity on the ice, from skaters poling themselves along to military maneuvers on frozen rivers. The crude skate described in Bishop Olaus's chronicle gradually altered its shape (Cat. #9), becoming a wooden sole with a metal blade inserted lengthwise into it. There is reason to believe that Holland first developed this type of skate, which consisted of a wooden foot-board with a thick plug set into the heel. The plug was inserted into the heel of the skater's wooden shoe, and the front of the boot-board was fastened around the ball of the foot with leather bands (Cat. #10). Most early skates have long blades that extend far in front of the foot, terminating in graceful upward curls tipped with balls or acorns for decoration (Cat. #11). English skaters improved upon the Dutch design, shortening the foot-boards and blades considerably.[13]

The invention of sharp, iron skates led to the first, and most elementary, skating step, the so-called "Dutch Roll." As the name suggests, this style of skating originated in Holland and required the skater to push diagonally backward on the inside edge of one skate while gliding forward on the outside edge of the other.[14] This method transformed skating from crude sliding to controlled, powerful gliding on the ice. The result was a relaxed, rocking style of skating, characterized by graceful curves on the outer edge following the natural direction of the blade. Dutch art abounds with promenading folk skating over city ice in this way, hands clasped behind their backs or interlocked with partners, leaning to the side on one foot or the other (Cat. #12, #27, #28, #43, #44, Fig. 6). This type of skating was, and is, beautiful and relaxing, but hardly flamboyant. The extravagant movements of modern figure skating were not possible without a firm uniting of skate and shoe. Though legend has it that the Russian Czar Peter the Great attached a pair of blades permanently to his boots, this innovation was not generally available to skaters until the mid-19th century. Thanks to the invention of the American E.V. Bushnell, it became possible to twist and turn with no fear of dislodging the skates, thus enabling skaters to attempt complex movements. The technical advances of skatemakers, combined with the graceful tradition of the "Dutch Roll," signaled the beginning of the modern art of ice dancing and figure skating.[15]

Another method of skating developed among the peasants and farmers of northern Holland. The so-called "Frisian School," or "Fries style" of skating, had speed as its object rather than elegance. This type of skating is the ancestor of modern speed skating, and required the skater to bend low and go straight ahead with all possible velocity (Cat. #13). Frisian farmers, bent on getting their produce to market as quickly as possible, developed a special type of skate to accommodate them. The blades were thick, blunt and broad, allowing for maximum stability of weight and long powerful strides. The advantage of rapid travel on the ice is reflected in the popular Dutch proverb: "...winter brings skaters farther than wagons do on the longest day of summer."[16] Eventually, the competitive spirit arose among the practical Frisians. Who could skate the farthest—the fastest? Races, which were known since the time of Bishop Olaus, became increasingly popular, developing into the modern Olympic sport of speed skating.

Early skaters were well-aware of the dangers involved in their activities on the ice. In both sport and recreational skating, they took practical precautions to avoid disaster and to deal with accidents. The long poles and ladders that appear with skaters in Dutch art attest to the caution that was routinely observed (Cat. #14). In fact, a modern issue of *Skating* magazine reproduces a photo that looks remarkably like the rescue attempt illustrated in Weigel's 17th century book, *Ethica Natuuralis seu documenta moralia* (Cat. #15). The modern photo caption describes the following procedure for "Rescuing a Fallen Comrade:" "The rescuer must first think how he can extend himself without getting into danger. This can be done by a ladder, plank or tree limb.... One of the better devices for rescue is a long, light pole with a looped end of line. When the rescuer can get close, the rope loop is dropped over the head and shoulders of the victim."[17] When not being used to fish fellow skaters out of icy water, such poles were convenient tools for testing the strength and thickness of ice. In art, these poles sometimes appear strapped onto the backs of skaters, where they were instantly accessible in case of emergency.

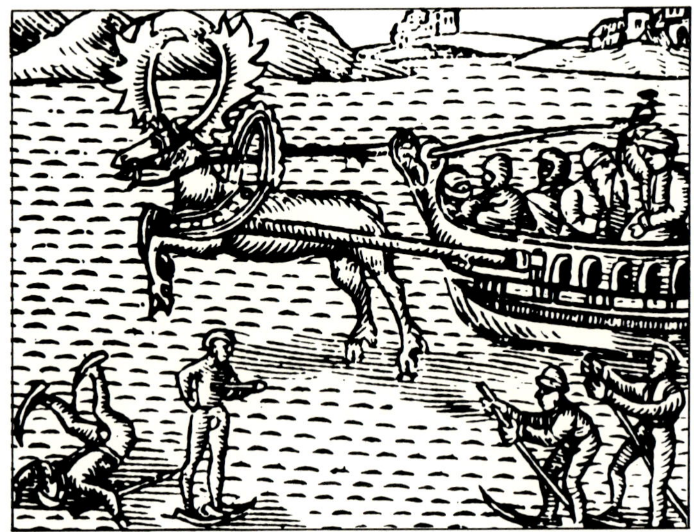

Cat. #8

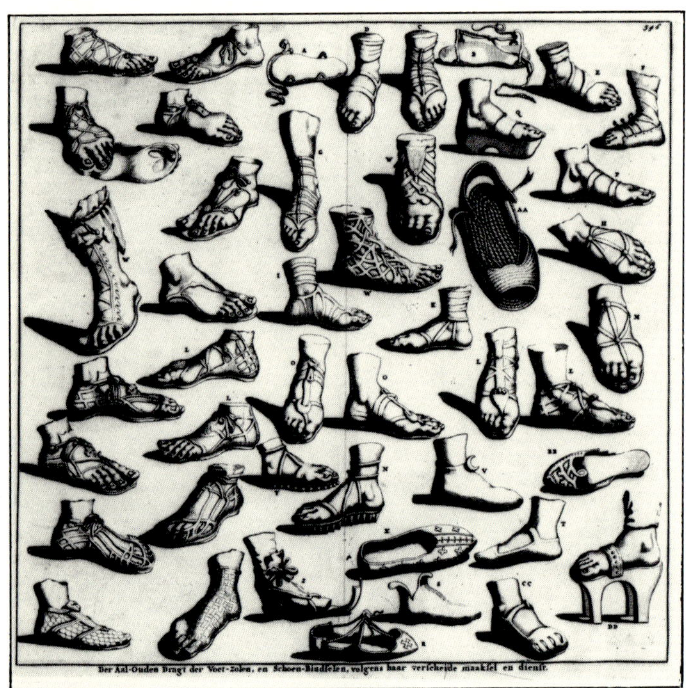

Cat. #9

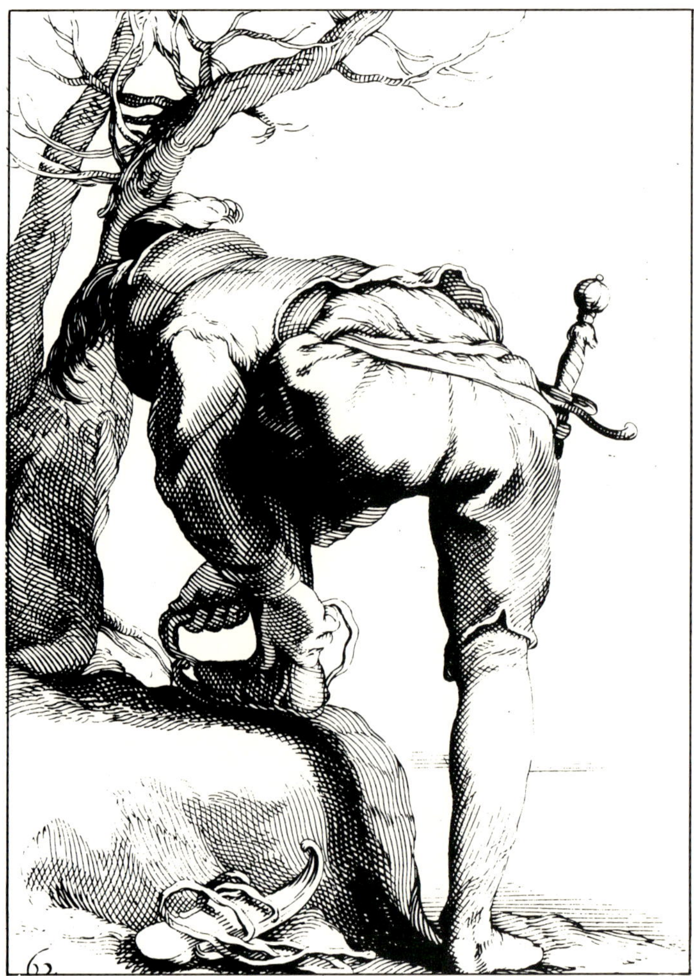

Cat. #10

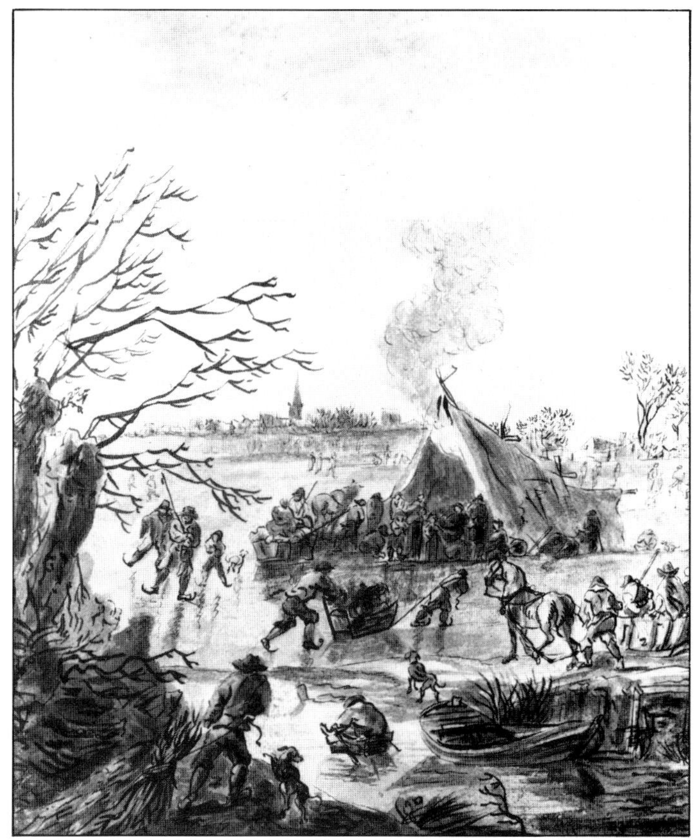

Cat. #12

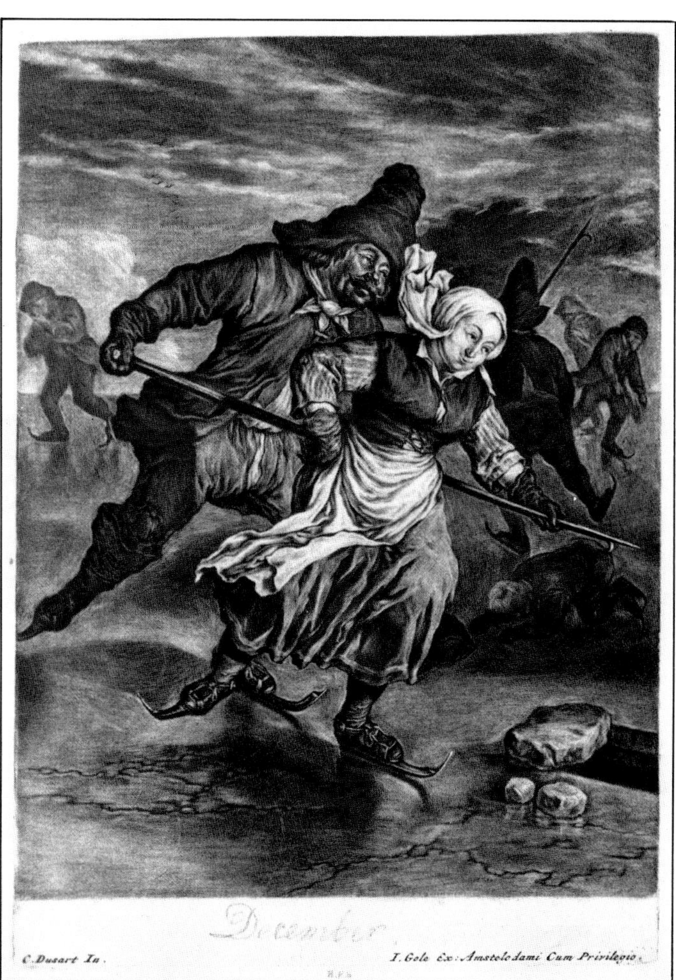

Cat. #13

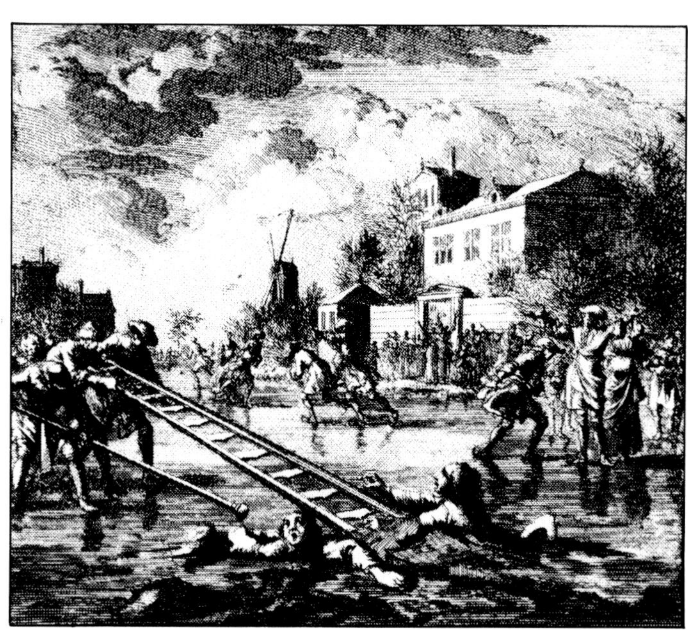

Cat. #15

GAMES ON THE ICE

Poles also had their playful uses. Dutch boys decorated them with colorful stripes and tassels at the ends, sometimes using them in boisterous competitive play. As early as 1180, Fitzstephen's chronicle notes: "Sometimes two (boys) runne together with poles, and hitting one the other, eyther one or both doe fall, not without hurt; some breake their armes, some their legs, but youth desirous of glorie, in this sort exerciseth it selfe against the time of warre."[18] Pole skating could save energy by allowing one of a group of skaters to catch his or her breath (Cat. #13, Fig. 6). When the person in front tired of being the windbreaker, he or she simply slid to the back, allowing the next in line to lead. Sometimes a stiff breeze blew from behind and the skating line could glide abreast, letting the wind do the work. Artists often depicted groups of young men and women gripping a wooden staff skating this way in single file.

Dutch art attests to the fun that groups of people had on the ice as skating took on a recreational aspect in addition to its practical one. Beginning with Pieter Bruegel the Elder, artists delighted in depicting the many forms of leisure skating, often with encyclopedic veracity (Cat. #1, #3, #16, #17). Children, who learned to skate before they could read, weave in and out of these scenes, sharing and sometimes invading the ice occupied by their parents and elders. Sometimes they play *ijsleete* or "ice sleds" (Cat. #40, #50), a popular children's game that involved large wood balls that were placed in rows several yards apart. The object was to pick up the balls, place them one by one on the sled and return to the starting point as quickly as possible without losing them. Older children sometimes dispensed with sleds altogether, gathering the balls on skates alone.[19] Younger children enjoyed playing with tops on the ice, which afforded a slick surface for optimum spin (Cat. #1).

Adults joined the fun, too. Often a sledder or a skater would be spun rapidly around in circles, held to a center post by a tether rope or spun by human effort (Cat. #16, #17). Rings of people would form around this activity, cheering the skater/sledder to ever more dizzying circles. Other games that can be identified in Dutch art were forerunners of modern sports, such as *eisschiessen*, the ancestor of curling (Cat. #18), and "bandy," a hockey-like team game played with sticks and balls. Occasionally, dozens of folk would join to play "snake," an early form of "crack the whip," where every attempt was made to avoid breaking the long line of people on skates (Cat. #19). "Kolf" was a popular Dutch ice sport that was adapted to dry land toward the end of the little ice age (Cat. #3, #20, #21). It involved hitting a small ball around an obstacle course with a long club (Fig. 2). We know it today by the only slightly Anglicized name of "golf."[20]

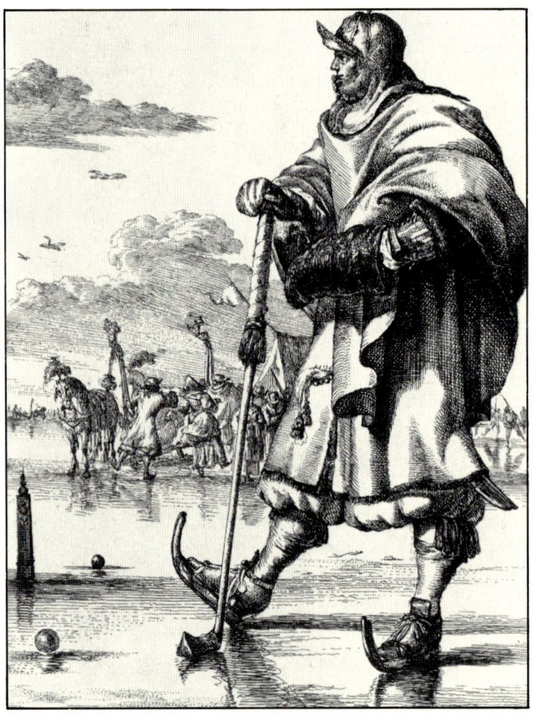

Figure 2 R. de Hooghe, *Golfer*, engr., (Amsterdam, Rijksprentenkabinet #1 8711)

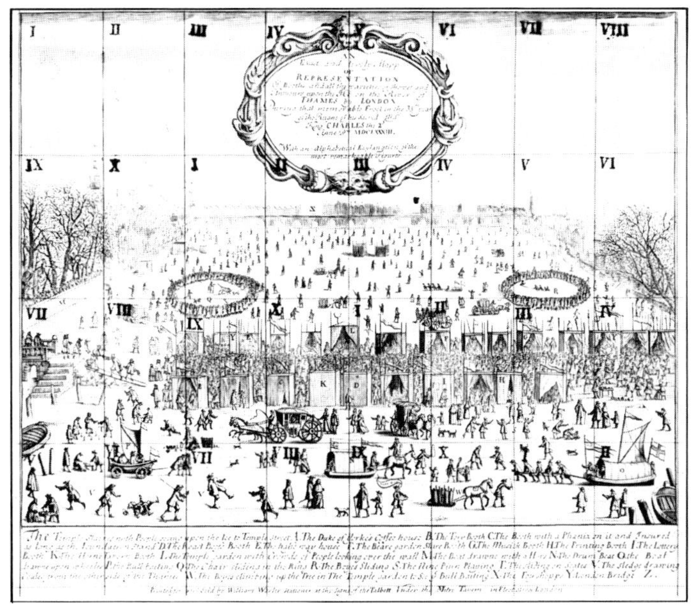

Cat. #16

HYEMS

Cat. #18

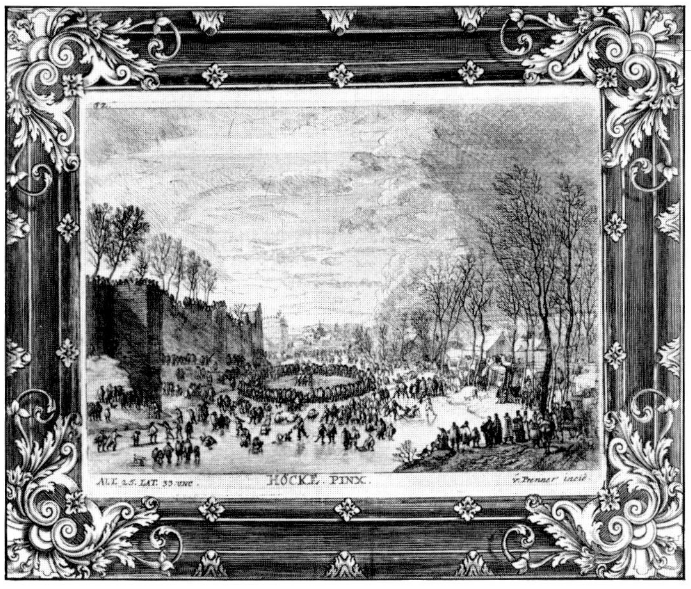

Cat. #17

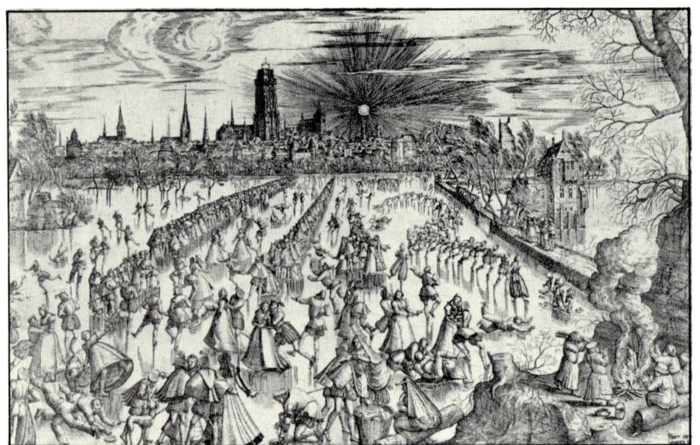

Cat. #19

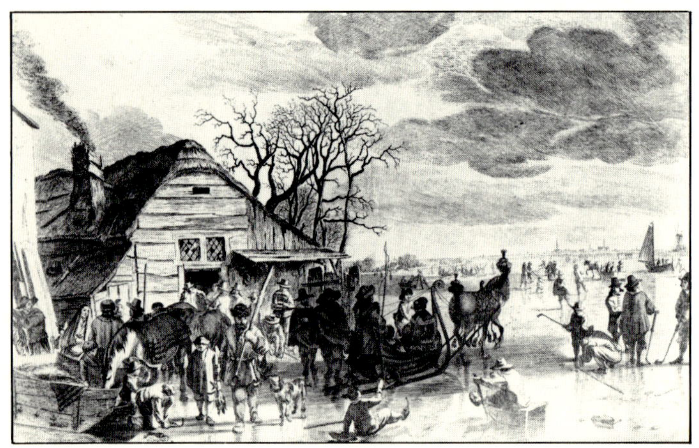

Cat. #20

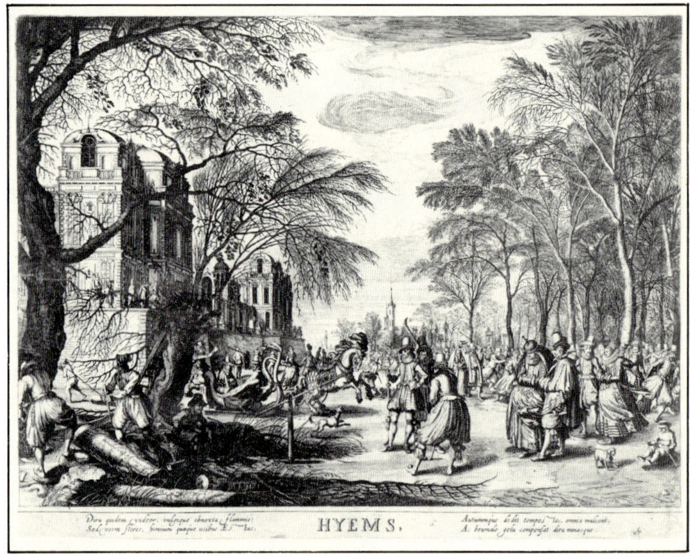

Cat. #21

THE NATIONAL SPORT OF HOLLAND

The word "skate" is derived from the Dutch word "schaats." It is not surprising then that skating was so much a part of the life, thought and art of 17th-century Holland, that the sport became synonymous with Dutch nationalism. People of all ages and social levels—from gentry to peasant—came together on the ice (Cat. #22, #23, #52). Like jogging is today, skating was an outdoor exercise that did not discriminate on account of age, sex or class. Once on the ice, the Dutch tended to disregard social status—royalty mixed with their subjects, men raced against women and senior citizens glided across the ice as easily as their grandchildren. All were equally likely to suffer the indignity of falling, and everyone could experience the exhilarating sense of freedom of gliding on skates.

Skating, then, was the perfect symbol for the system of democratic elective government that distinguished the United Provinces from the less egalitarian monarchies that ruled the rest of the world.[21] As such, ice skating often figures prominently in images of Dutch cities (Cat. #24, #25) or in atlases illustrating "Holland." Sometimes the city skyline appears with crowds of thrifty, hard-working people milling before it. Other scenes feature famous city buildings, such as the Customs House at Amsterdam (Cat. #26) or the castle at Zuylen (Cat. #27), where the civic virtues signified by the architecture are mirrored by the industrious folk milling about near it. The dedicatory Latin verse accompanying Jan van der Velde's *January* (Cat. #28) reflects the image above it: "Grassy rivers bound by ice are everywhere inscribed by the iron-shod feet of boys, choruses of young men, and processions of teasing, merry maidens." These words mirror the artistic and economic image of the Hague, distinguished by the city's affluent residents promenading upon its main canal.

In the same spirit of Dutch pride, van Sichem's engraving of the *Ice Ship* (Fig. 3) lauds the invention of a "boat that sails on frozen ice and slippery land." The lengthy inscription explains how the ice ship, loaded with people, can sail seven miles in two hours. The boastful words continue to describe the Dutch as braver, better soldiers in the war with Spain, better navigators and, of course, better skaters. The patriotic message of this image and others like it implies that, in Holland, a prosperous life could be attained in the same manner as proficiency in skating—by courage, hard work and determination rather than by accident of birth.

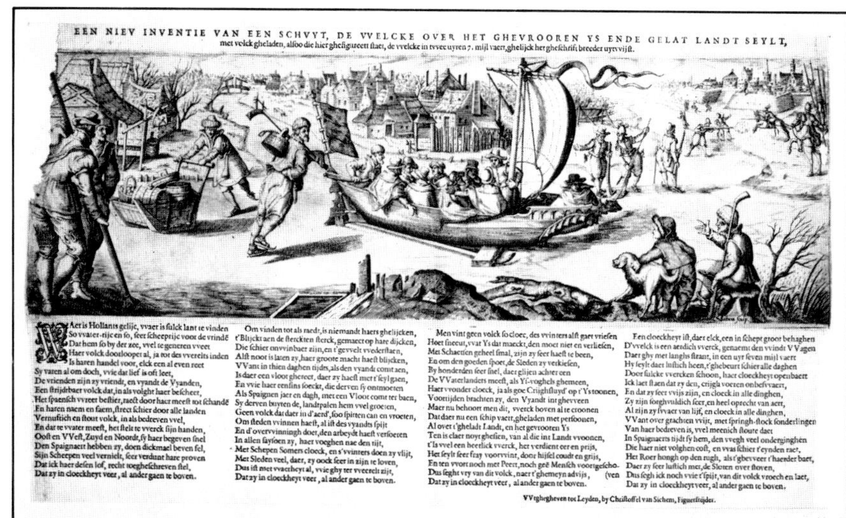

Figure 3 C. van Sichem, *The Ice Ship*, engr. (Amsterdam, Rijksprentenkabinet #A 19368)

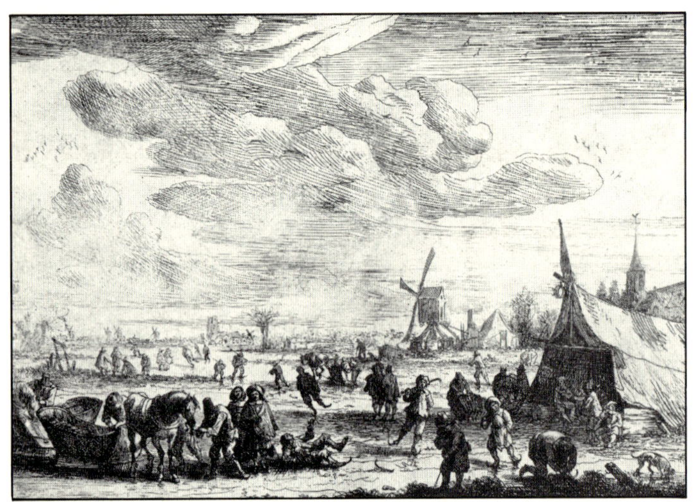

Cat. #22

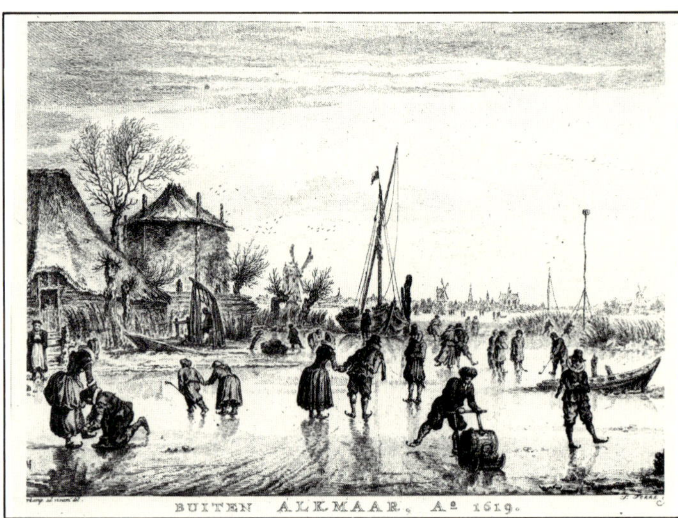

Cat. #24

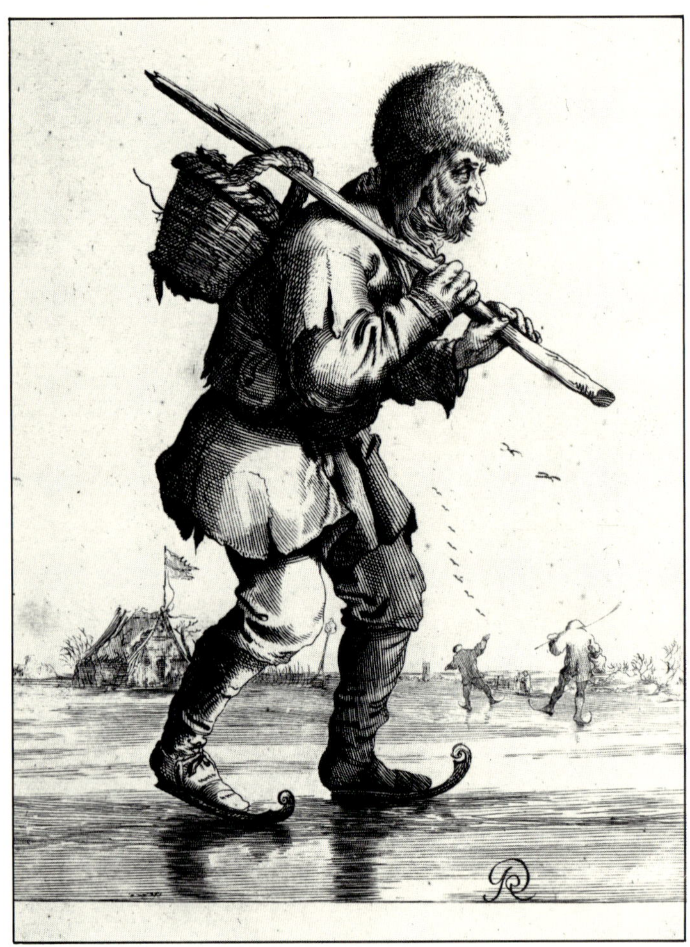

Cat. #23

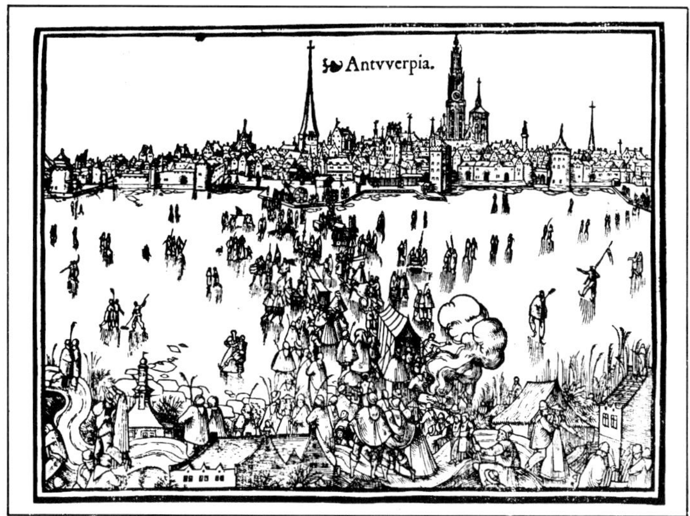

Cat. #25

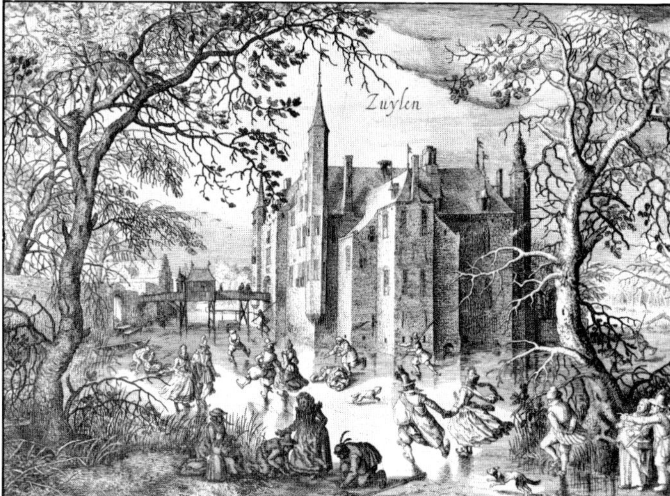

Cat. #27

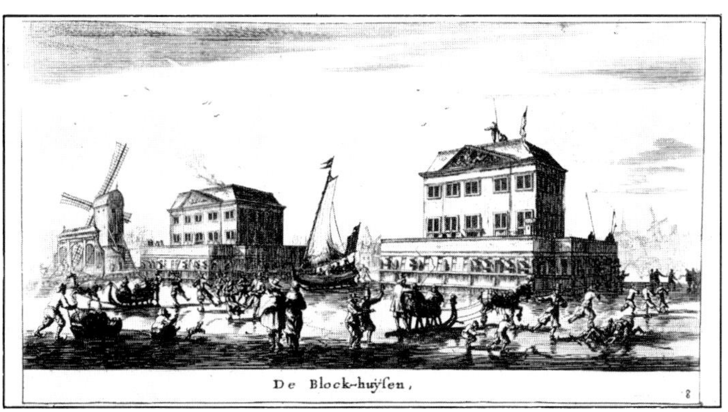

Cat. #26

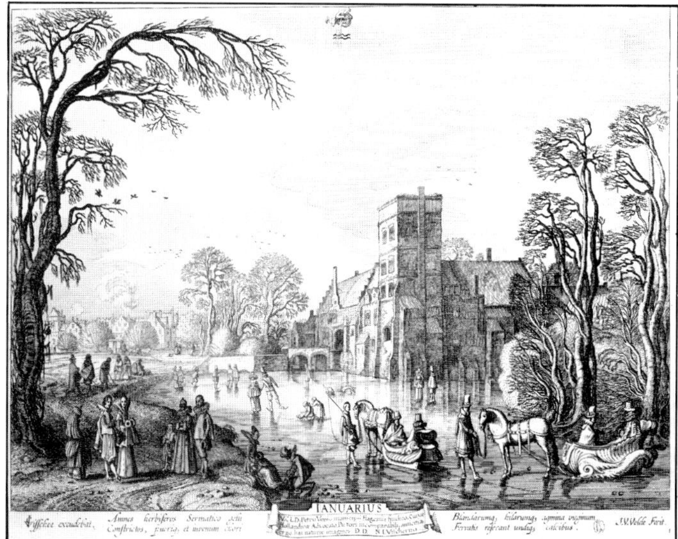

Cat. #28

Skating As Allegory

Thinking in riddles and double allusions was a way of life before the Industrial Revolution ushered in the pragmatism of the technological age. It is not surprising then that ice skating became the subject of many proverbs and sayings in the Dutch tradition and,

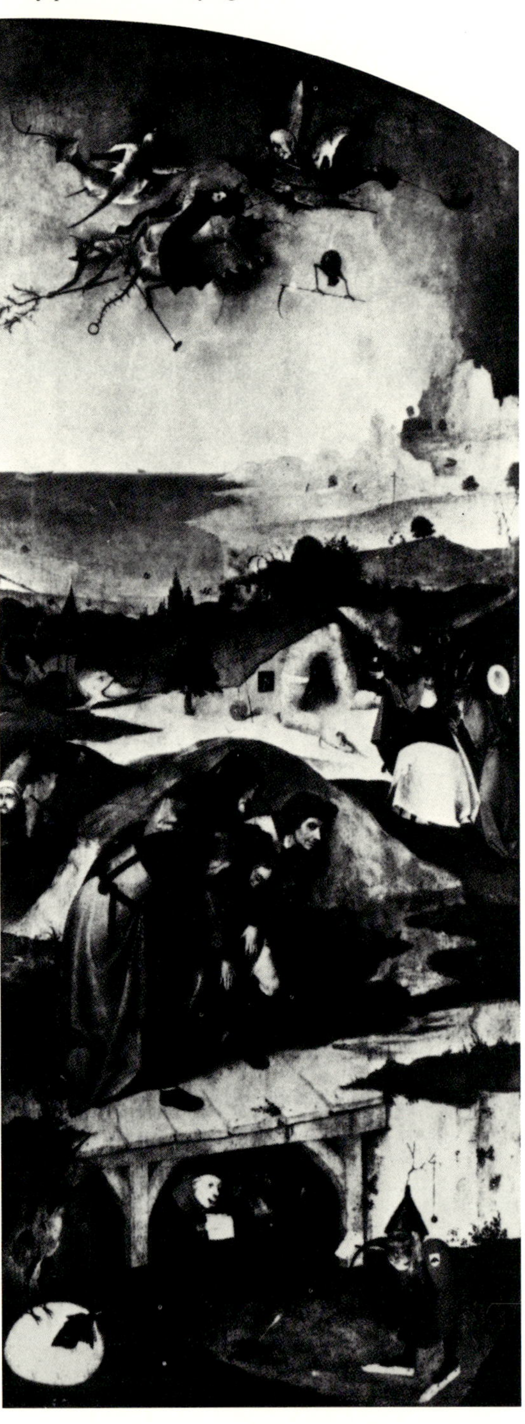

Figure 4 H. Bosch, *St. Anthony* triptych, left interior panel, c. 1500 (Lisbon, National Museum of Art)

as a result, took on symbolic meaning in Dutch art. For example, the saying "skating on thin ice," which most people would identify as an American proverb, is only one of many popular sayings about skating that our culture retains as a remnant of the Dutch colonization of North America. In a single phrase, the understandable risks of skating on a weak surface, through which one could possibly fall, are transferred to precarious life experiences. Other popular sayings apply the image of skating in the same way. For example, "I stand on cracking ice" meant that things were not going well; to "lead someone onto ice" meant to bring someone into a dangerous position; to "go on skates" meant to go wrong; and to ask someone why he or she was wearing wooden shoes on the ice meant that the person in question was asking for trouble.[22] Learning to balance, becoming proficient, gaining a bit too much confidence, taking unsafe risks and finally falling are the familiar patterns of human existence and became the objects of many clever sayings incorporating skating as a mirror of life.

The Dutch painter Hieronymus Bosch was one of the earliest artists to treat skating in a moralistic way. The beaked, dog-eared monster in the lower right corner of the left wing of the *St. Anthony* triptych (c. 1500), for example, wears a pair of skates (Fig. 4).[23] The inverted funnel atop its head indicates that the creature probably represents the folly of false alchemists who, in misguided efforts to find the "philosopher's stone," trod the uncertain ice of questionable laboratory practices.[24] Bosch intended that this image be equated with misguided folly. 17th-century artists, building on this precedent, treated skating as a microcosm that mirrored the macrocosm of daily life—warning of evil in the world and cautioning against wayward fate.

WINTER

Before the invention of inside rinks, ice skating could only be accomplished out-of-doors and then only in weather cold enough to firmly freeze several inches of water. It is no wonder that during the little ice age, the activity of skating became inseparable from the idea of "Winter." To 17th century people, however, winter conjured up a host of associated meanings that are not part of the modern awareness. Some of these associations came from Classical literature—others were religious in nature. There were many iconographic traditions that incorporated images of winter, among them, astrology, the labors of the months, the four humours and elements, and the corresponding four stages of the human life cycle. During the little ice age, representations of winter, no matter what the specific iconography, were likely to include skating as an accessory.

The 17th century was an era of rapidly changing scientific awareness. Though Galileo's earth-centered universe was by now an accepted fact, the ancient astrological belief in the zodiac and its influence over human life held fast in scientific circles.[25] Among the earliest astrological works of art to show a full-fledged outdoor winter landscape is the month of "February" from the *Très Riches Heures* of the Limbourg brothers (c. 1400) (Fig. 5). The scene shows peasants warming themselves inside a cutaway view of their cramped hovel while sheep huddle in an outdoor shelter. Above, in a semi-circular painted tympanum, the zodiac signs that share the month of February make their circuit across the sky—Aquarius the water-bearer begins at the left side, and the two fishes of Pisces curve off to the right. The united image of the celestial and terrestrial worlds epitomizes the medieval belief in the unity of nature and humanity. Following this precedent, the traditional labors of the winter months became common subjects for 17th century artists. Stevens's engraving of *Winter* (Cat. #29), for example, show wood-gathering, an activity that was practiced in January in preparation for the cold months ahead.

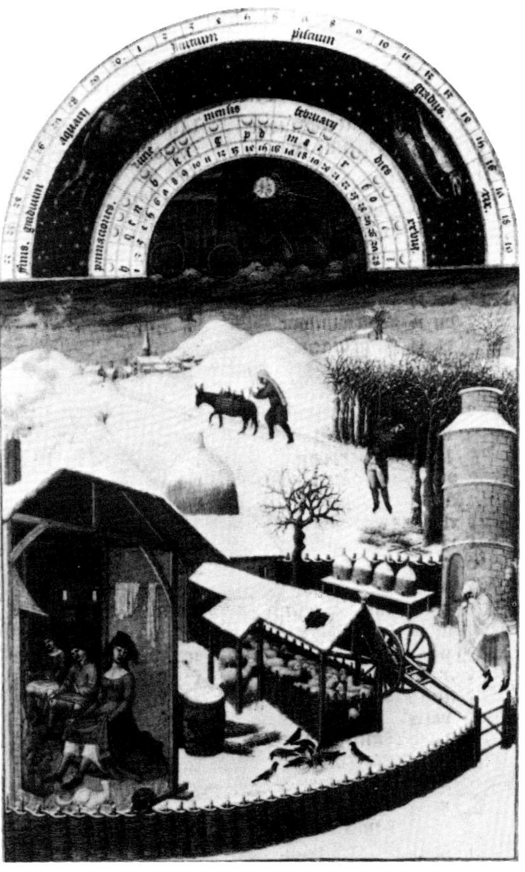

Figure 5 Limbourg Brothers, "February" from the *Très Riches Heures* (Chantilly, Musée Condé)

Ice skating is also an important part of scenes that portray winter church festivals, such as Christmas and Epiphany, also called Twelfth Night or the Feast of the Magi. This artistic tradition dates at least to the late 14th century, when manuscript illuminators depicted the birth and infancy of Christ as taking place amid winter surroundings. The holiday spirit of winter is captured in Crispijn de Passe's engraving of Twelfth Night revelers (Cat. #30). Here, the astrological sign of Aquarius appears in the sky above a group of cavorting skaters, marking the date of the festival, January 6. Similarly, the night sky in Matham's

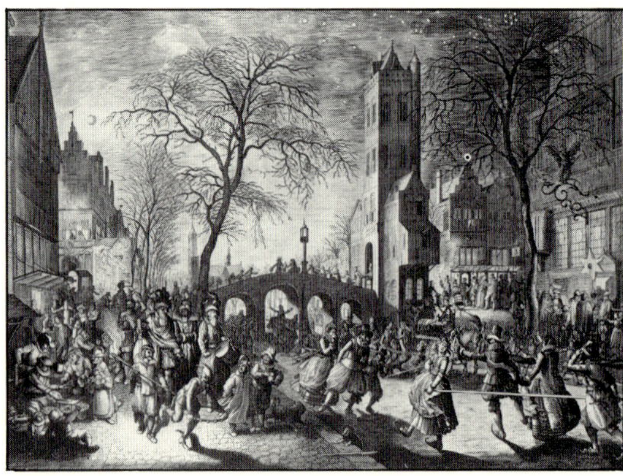

Driekoningenavond clearly shows a view of the heavens that can still be seen during the holiday season (Fig. 6). Stars forming the zodiacal configurations of Capricorn and Aquarius glow above city buildings and canals teeming with Twelfth Night revelers on skates.

The many faces of winter included some that were secular in origin. The anonymous "Master A.P" combined several of these traditions in his engraving of *Hyems* (Winter) (Fig. 7). "Hyems," symbolized by an old woman balancing a smoking cauldron on her head, stands in the middle of the winter spectacle. The zodiac signs of Capricorn, Aquarius and Pisces appear on flags above the crowd while plaques bearing the corresponding names of the winter months— December, January and February—appear tied to the midsections of the zodiacal flagposts. Other characters associated with winter are labeled with their names. "Eolus," god of winds, strides off to the left while

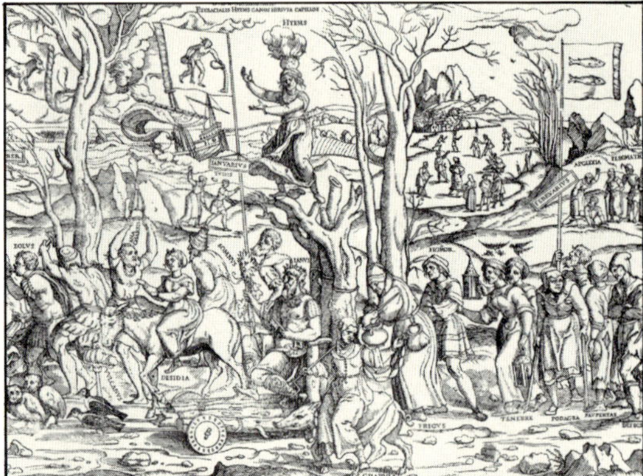

"Janus," the two-faced god who welcomes the new year and bids the old goodbye, sits just left of center. These two share the scene with other figures who personify the human attributes of the winter season— unsavory looking characters with names like "crapula" (intoxication), "tenebre" (darkness) and "defectus" (failure). All are figures borrowed from classical mythology and the writings of Ovid.

The Master A.P. reflected scientific tradition as well as Classical revivalism in his engraving of *Hyems*. Early medical science recognized four physical types— the sanguine, choleric, melancholic and phlegmatic— that corresponded to the four elements (air, fire, earth and water), seasons (spring, summer, fall, winter) and phases of the human life cycle (childhood, youth, middle age, senility).[26] The unfortunate "phlegmatic" type was ruled by cold, wetness and the season of winter. This humour was characterized by old age and the infirmities that often plague this time of life. The Master A.P.'s engraving includes, among the ice skaters in the right background, a little group of old folk leaning on canes beneath the zodiac flag of Pisces. They are labeled "plegmatici" and represent the humour associated with winter. In the same way, 17th century artistic representations of winter, which often combined both old folk and ice skaters, can also be interpreted as allegories of old age.

"Old Man Winter" was a popular subject for 17th century artists. Sadeler's engraving after Barendsz shows an old man warming his hands and feet before a fire as a figure on skates is glimpsed in the background (Cat. #31). The caption at the bottom links the season with its human correspondent: "How well do winter and sad old age tally. One takes the beauty of the bloom, the other, the glory of youth...each created thing awaits its end." In the same tradition, Sadeler's engraving after Heinrich Bol places the old man amid a bustle of winter activities—skaters, butchers and fuel-gatherers carry on with their lives beneath the three zodiac signs of winter (Cat. #32). The accompanying inscription warns: "...Winter takes the pleasant dish provided by earlier effort with virile hand. Whoever in such a way provides for himself while his years are intact, will pass happily the hard times of old age." Indeed, the frivolous play of the skaters in the right sector of the scene contrasts starkly with the serious workers depicted in the left. 17th century viewers were encouraged to emulate "Old Man Winter," whose healthy fire and well-stocked table indicate that he provided for his retirement during the springtime of his youth.

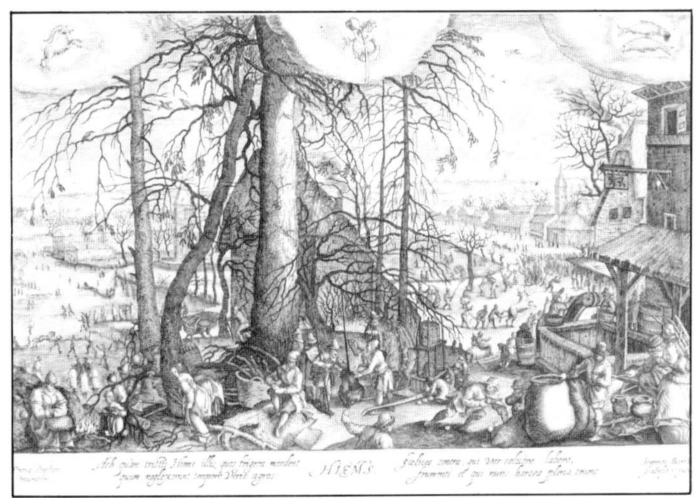

Cat. #29

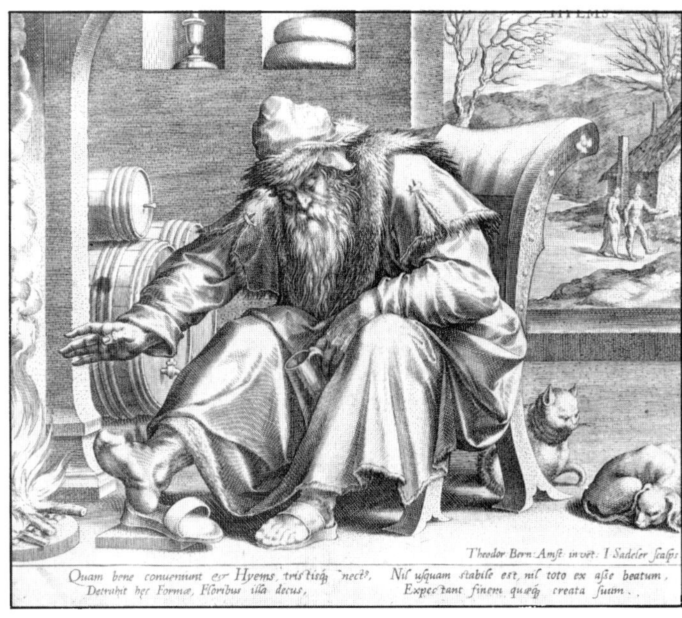

Cat. #31

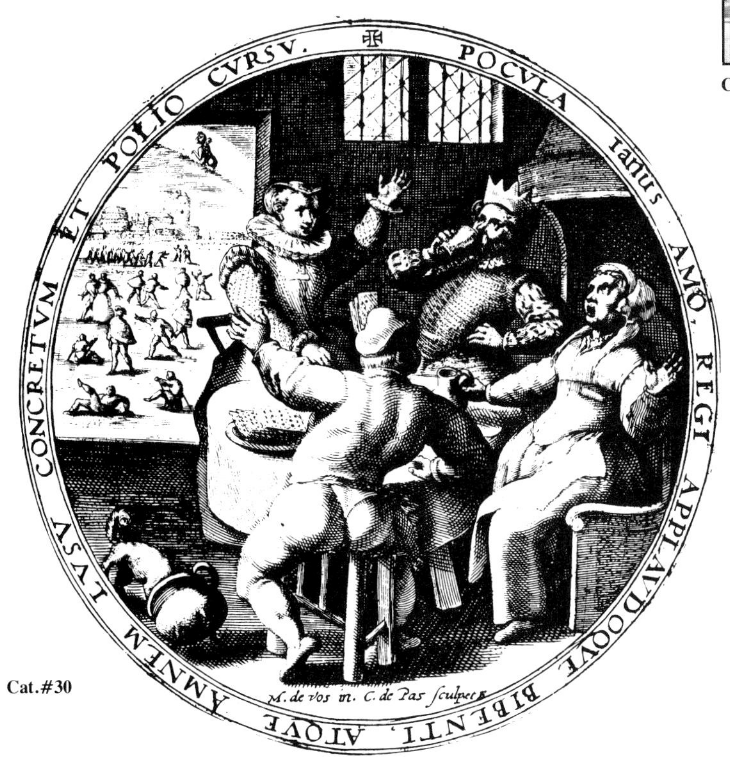

Cat.#30

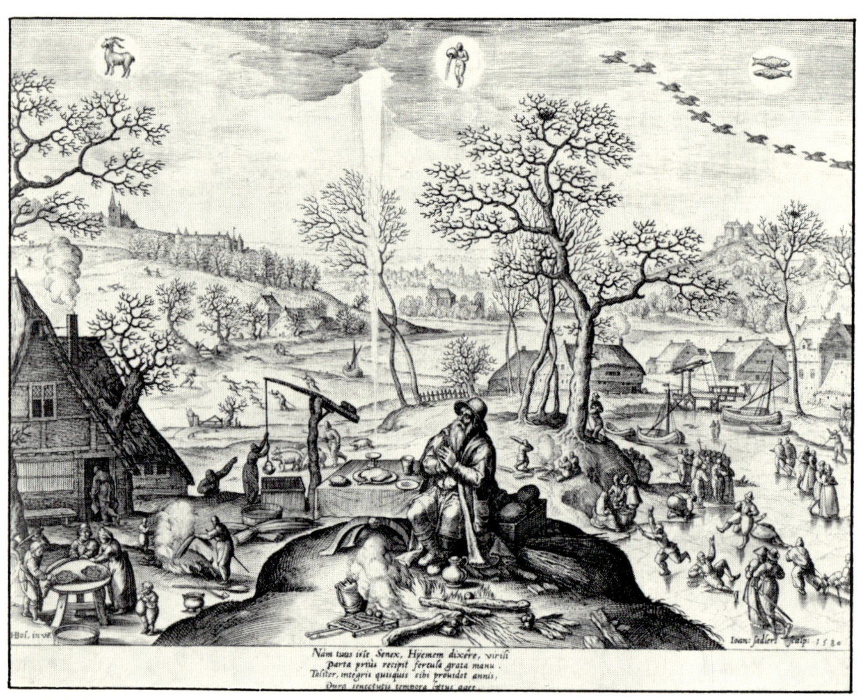

Bol. inuen.
Ioan: Sadler. sculp: 1580.
Nàm tuus iste Senex, Hyemem dixere, virili
parta priùs recipit fercula grata manu.
Taliter, integris quisquis sibi prouidet annis,
Onera senectutis tempora lætus agit.

Cat. #32

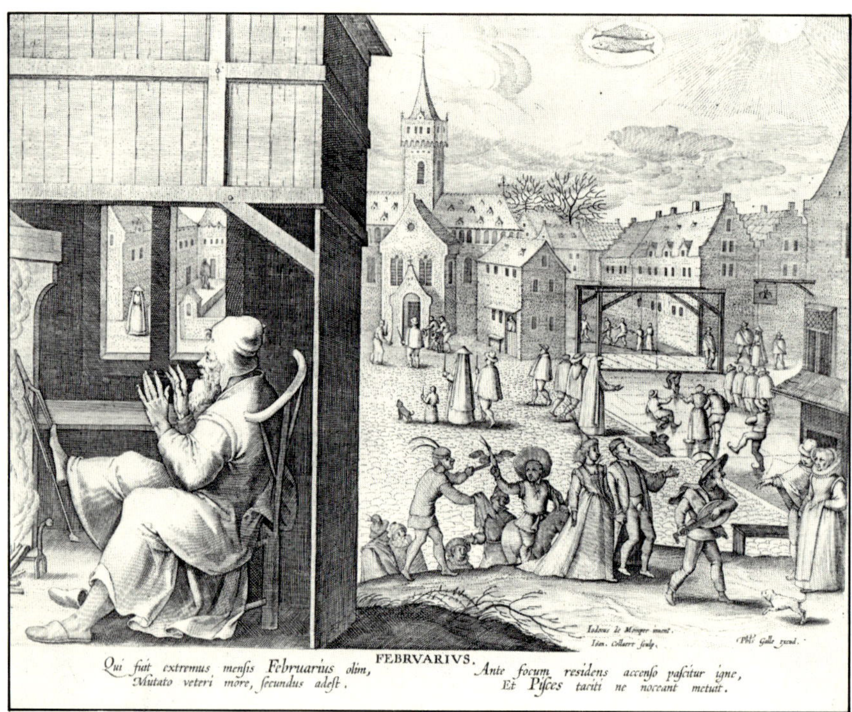

Iodocus de Mompere inuent.
Ioan. Collaert sculp.
Phls Galle excud.
FEBRVARIVS.
Qui fuit extremus mensis Februarius olim,
Mutato veteri more, secundus adest.
Ante focum residens accenso pascitur igne,
Et Pisces taciti ne noceant metuit.

Cat. #33

SKATING EMBLEMS

The earliest image of skating is a religious one and illustrates the life of St. Lydwine of Schiedam, patron saint of skaters (Cat. #34).[27] A page from her biography, written by Jean Brugman in 1498, shows Lydwine collapsed on the ice and supported by two female companions—martyred in a skating accident. Behind her a young man calmly performs the "Dutch Roll," oblivious to the miracle that is happening before him. Christian legend relates that Lydwine, a beautiful and virtuous girl from the Dutch town of Schiedam, was encouraged to go skating for the sake of her delicate health. While negotiating some rough ice, she was accidentally knocked down by one of her friends, breaking a rib on her right side. In the year 1396, physicians were not as well-practiced in setting bones as they are today, so poor Lydwine became an invalid, a martyr to unspeakable pains and torments that she bore with fortitude. Visions and miracles marked the rest of her days, during which she reportedly neither ate nor drank. The pious Lydwine died in 1433 and was beatified in 1890. Her relics were given to a Carmelite monastery in Brussels.[28] To 15th century Catholics, Lydwine's martyrdom signified more than an unfortunate tale of pain and sorrow. Her accident was interpreted as a symbol of evil in an uncertain world,[29] and the slippery ice on which she fell implied the waywardness of fate.

17th century emblem books, in the same tradition as the illustrator of Brugman's *Vita Lydwine*, related the perils of skating to the obstacles of life. The content of these books, which reached the peak of their popularity in the early and mid-17th century, combined Classical texts, passages from the Bible and popular proverbs in the form of moralizing poems illustrated by symbolic images.[30] Readers would entertain themselves by guessing the meanings of these cryptic images before reading the accompanying texts. Likewise, artists would include familiar emblem images in their paintings, there to be "discovered" by observant viewers, who would then supply the missing proverbial texts. Recent scholarship has concentrated primarily on the preponderance of emblematic images in Dutch art,[31] even though the texts of these books usually appeared in several languages. This attests to the sophisticated international nature of the upper strata of 17th century Dutch society, where children were often taught the rudiments of Latin and French before studying their own language. This talent for linguistics, a remnant of the 17th century Dutch involvement in international trade, remains a remarkable characteristic of the Dutch people.

Emblem books demonstrate a unity of text and image unprecedented in the history of art. Scenes from daily life, allegorical fantasies and humorous vignettes take on new meaning when viewed in the context of the accompanying texts. Such is the case with the *Spiegel van het Manselijk Bedrijf*, or *The Mirror of Human Occupations* (Cat. #35), which portrays every aspect of 17th century Dutch work and employment, from farmers and sailmakers to doctors and lawyers. The "Skatemaker" illustrates a man hard at work sharpening a blade while a customer waits at the open window. This image, which at first glance appears to be a staid depiction of the Protestant work ethic, is revealed, upon reading the text, to be an admonition against frivolity. The caption above says: "For idle pleasure, A risk of measure." The text beneath explains: "The folly to seek pleasure's fruit, While mankind pleasure-seeking must—Leads people on the water's crust, and lets death gape from underfoot: Thus is man caught in earthly spell, while underneath gapes the gate of hell." The equation of skating and death is more obvious in S. van Rusting's *Het Schouw-Toneel des Doods*...(Dance of Death) (Cat. #36), where skaters glide along the ice followed by a skeleton who mimics their movements. The text adds to the macabre visual *memento mori* by admonishing: "Courage! Ho! Death is on their Heels.... How lightly ventures man, carefree, On ice, not thinking deeper! And so he is an inch or three Ahead of the Big Reaper." Death is linked with original sin in David's *Christeliicke Waerseggher* (Cat. #37), which pictures Eve holding a skull, bound to a barren tree by the coils of Satan's tail. Behind her, a man bursts into flame and a skater falls through the ice. The Latin, Dutch and French texts all ask the same question: "What is that strange evil that taints us so?" The answer, of course, is "Sin; and temptation that beckons us." The message also appears at the top of the page: "Sin and its occasion must be avoided."

Caution in life is often the hidden message of emblem texts and images. An illustration from Rollenhagius's *Selectorum emblematum centuria secunda*...(Cat. #38) shows a traveler embarking on a journey down a frozen canal. The inscription beneath warns to "make haste slowly:" "I pass across the ice cautiously step by step; he who hastens slowly, he who is slowly discerning, that man is wise...." Likewise, emblem 19 from Bèze's *Icones*...(Cat. #39) reminds us of the familiar "thin ice" saying: "He that dares support his weight on ice of frozen river, often perishes when the ice gives way. Learn by this example the fate of all whom, in countless ways, all life's treacherous boons deceive." Falling on ice is equated with life's inevitable reverses in Taurellus's *Emblemata psychico-ethica* (Cat. #40). The familiar image of playful boys sliding, poling and falling on ice is accompanied by a text that, first describes the harshness of winter capable of freezing even the greatest rivers. The cautionary words continue: "Prepare thy heart for any chance misstep, should fate afflict thee with a weightier woe; thus irreparable be thy life's ordered plan." In the same way, two emblems from a German book equate the difficulties of walking on stilts and staying upright on ice to maintaining balance in life (Cat. #41).

Emblems were not always so pessimistic. Even old age could reveal hope, as Jacob Cats's *Houwelick* ...(Marriage) (Cat. #42), showing an old woman warming herself on a snow-covered bank, implies. In the background, a young girl nimbly cavorts with her lover on the ice. Though frankly sexist by today's enlightened expectations of mature womanhood, Cats's illustration of the "widowed housewife" was intended to impart soothing words of comfort to 17th century women: "...Here comes old Time, with wintry and cold days, Gone is youth, and so the summer ways. There is no other course: the inner forces grow, To a new springtime and a summer glow." Parental duty was another aspect of domestic life that was compared to skating. The lyrics to a popular Dutch song published in a book illustrated with emblematic images (Cat. #43) say: "The sweetest pastime for me is in gliding, On skates from here to out in space: But to prevent this small girl's sliding, I watch her, meanwhile keeping pace." The song provides a model for responsible parenthood in lyrics that describe the watchful care of children on the ice.

Roemer Visscher's emblem book, *Sinnepoppen* (Cat. #44, #45), embodies another philosophical message in two illustrations of skaters. One depicts a skater expertly gliding along the ice accompanied by a verbal reminder that "practice makes perfect." Another image in the same book shows a man who has fallen on the ice and hit his head against a large stone in the foreground. The accompanying text is titled "In need of a Master" and continues: "There is nothing new about skating, that when a man falls down, he must get up again and act as if nothing had happened: in other words one should not be discouraged by adversity.... One thinks with the alchemist: once more it should be tried, accidentally it will happen. And when everything goes wrong again, one should move on...." The folly of those who do not apply the lessons of skating to their lives is illustrated in Cats's *Spiegel van den ouden en nieuwen tijt* (Cat. #46), where folk try to prod a donkey to stand on ice that cracks beneath its weight. The short, yet pithy inscription says merely: "When the donkey is in a good mood, he wants to dance on ice." This may be read as an admonishment against over-confident fools—asses who would dance on ice.

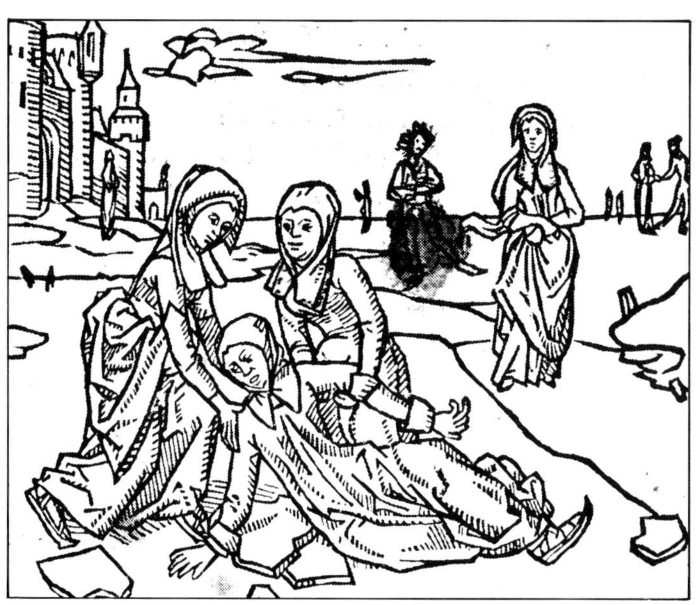

Cat. #34

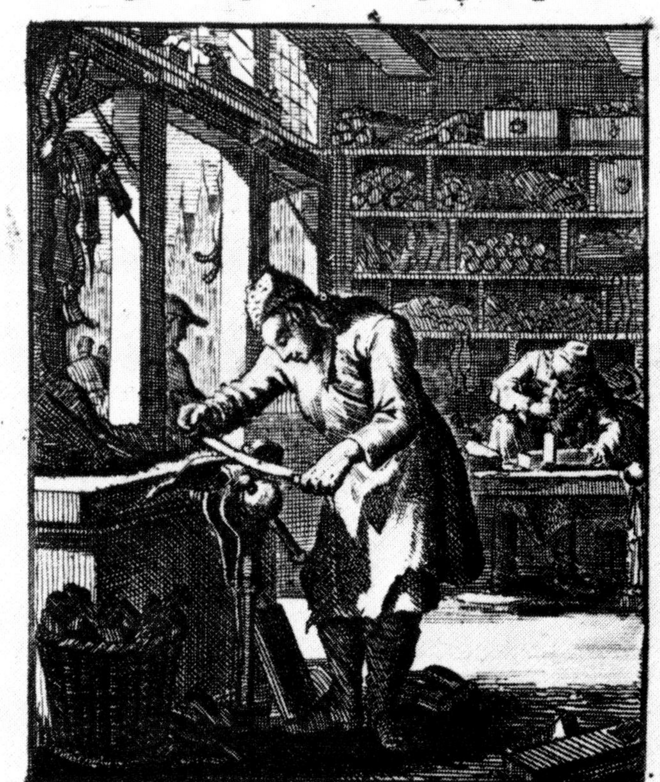

MENSELYK BEDRYF.   69
DE SCHAATSEMAAKER.
Om ligt behaagen, Een wigtig waagen.
De idelheid om vreugd te raapen
    Wyl 's werelds hert naar uitvlucht dorſt,
    Begeeft zich op de waterkorſt,
En laat de dood van onder gaapen :
    Zo ſpeelt de mens op 't aardſe wel,
    Als over 't gaapen van de hel.
                              Eze-

Cat. #35

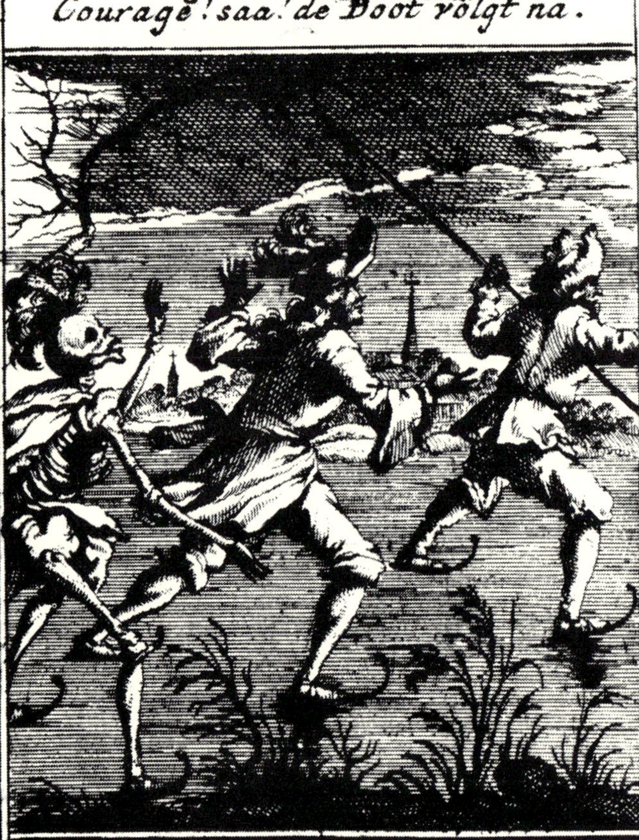

DOODEN DANS;
Verbeeldende SCHAATSE RYDERS.
Negen-en-twintigste Plaat.
Courage! saa, de Doot volgt na.

Hoe ligtlyk waagt men lyf en leven
Op 't ys, om kortswyl, zonder noot!
En dus bevint men zig pas even
Een duym twee drie maar van de Doot.

Cat. #36

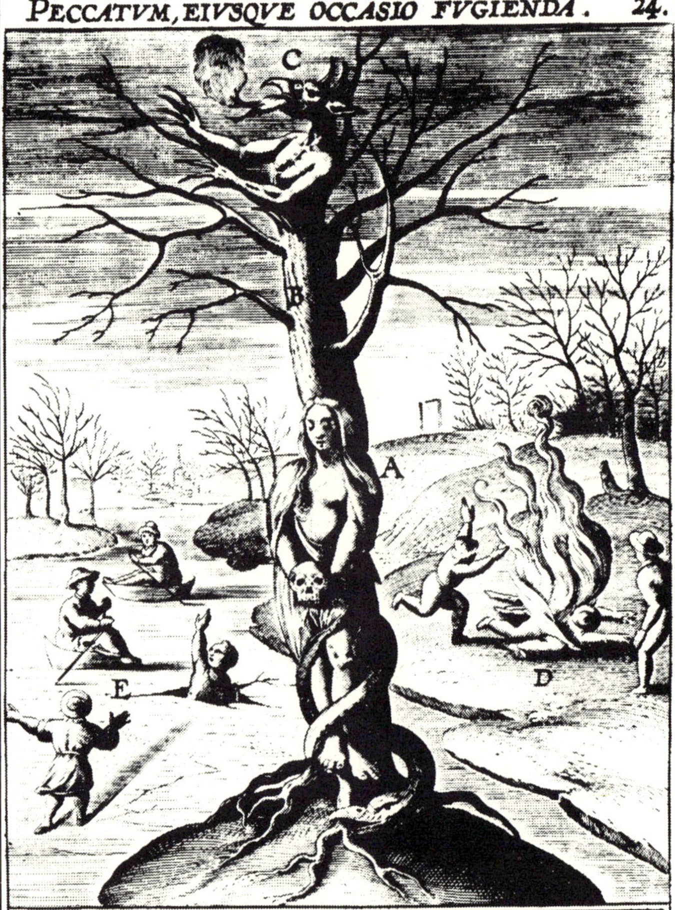

PECCATVM, EIVSQVE OCCASIO FVGIENDA. 24.

Quæ fugienda mihi mala sunt, cane peius, et angue?
Peccatum: Et quidquid peccato porrigit Ansam.

Welk is dat selsaem quaet; dat ons soo seer bevlekt?
De sonde; en alsulks saet, dat ons tot sonde trekt.

Quel mal veus tu peindre, Qui soit tant a craindre, Plus que nuls tormens?
Peché: et en somme, Ce qui tire l'homme, Aux debordemens

Cat. #37

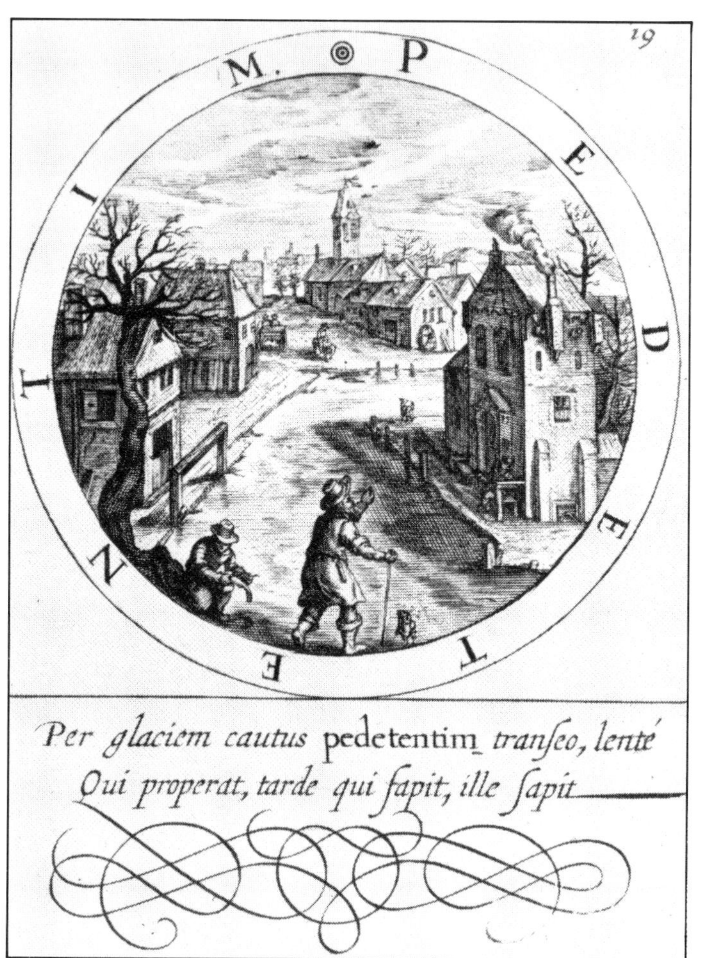

Per glaciem cautus pedetentim transeo, lenté
Qui properat, tarde qui sapit, ille sapit

Cat. #38

EMBLEMA XIX.

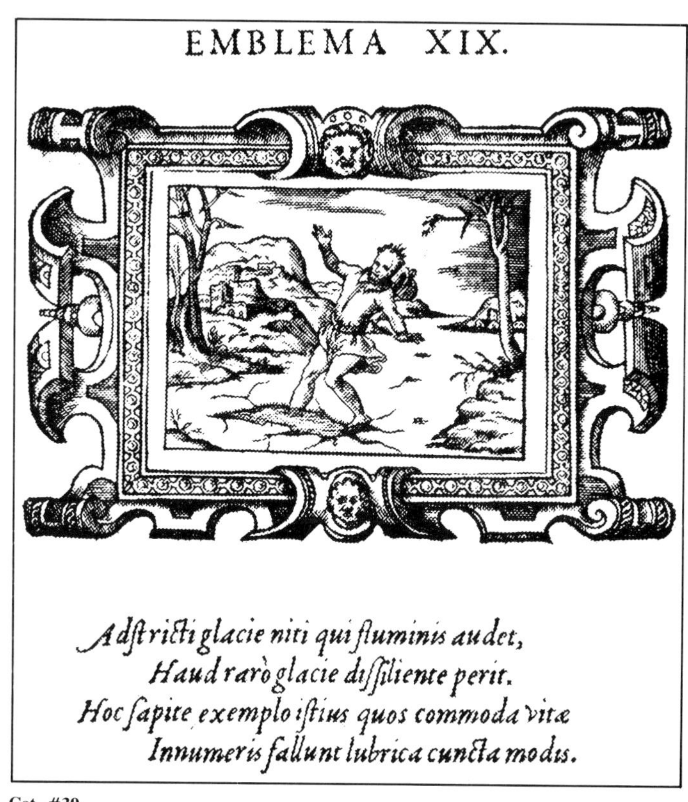

Adstricti glacie niti qui fluminis audet,
Haud raró glacie dissiliente perit.
Hoc sapite exemplo istius quos commoda vitæ
Innumeris fallunt lubrica cuncta modis.

Cat. #39

Frigore consistunt densata.

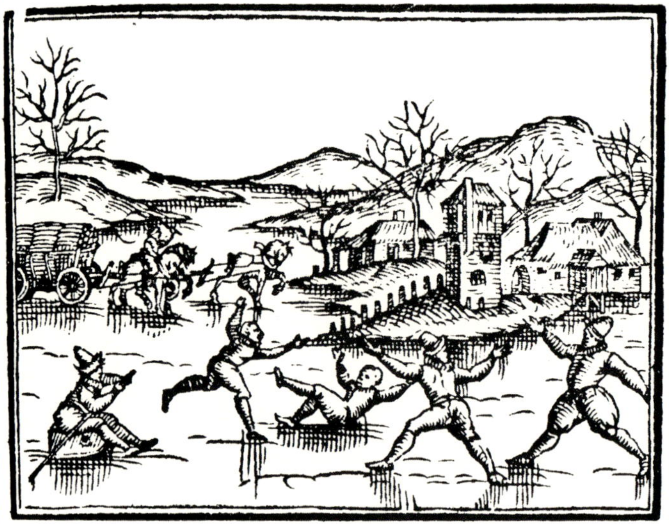

Maxima condensat penetrabile flumina frigus:
   Quin & consistunt frigiditate nives.
Hæcque sua tantò constantius omnia mole,
   Frigora quô fuerint asperiora, manent.
    Si fortuna tuis rebus iniquior
    Te duris agitet casibus anxium:
    His confide malis, quæ stabili tuum
    Ad quidvis animum robore comparant:
    Si sors afficiat te gravioribus:
    Ut vita ratio est irreparabilis.

Cat. #40

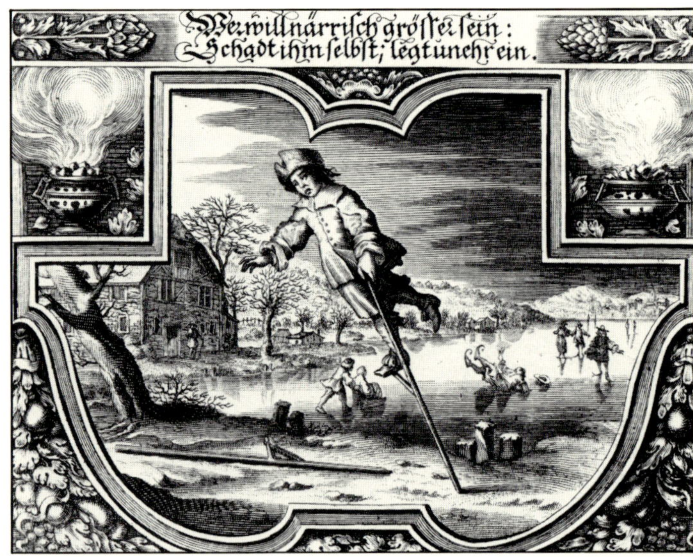

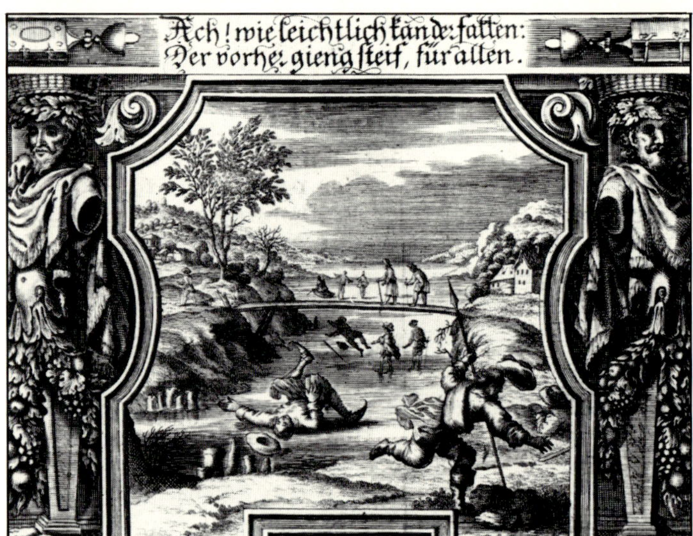

Cat. #41

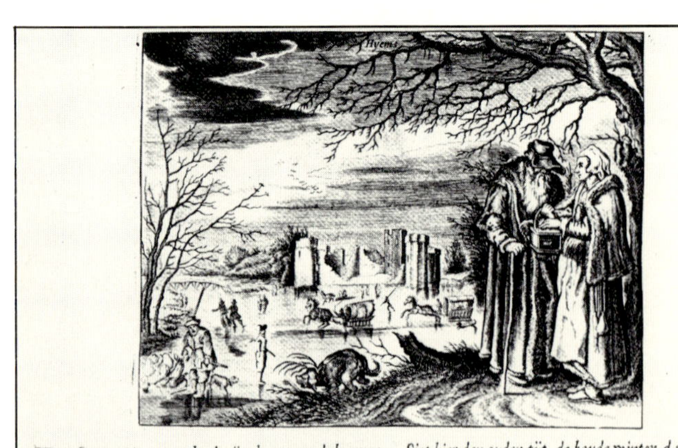

DE strenge winter naeckt, de rijm hangt aen de boomen,   *Siet hier den ouden tijt, de koude winter-dagen,*
De vorst verslint het groen, en bint de snelle stroomen;   *Verscheyden van de jeught, en van de somer-vlagen*
Men siet, gelijck het schijnt, geen leven in het kruyt,   *Hier is geen ander raet, als dat de binne-kracht*
Daer komt nochtans een dag, wanneer h. t weder spruyt.   *Een beter lente-tijt, een nieuwen somer wacht.*

Cat. #42

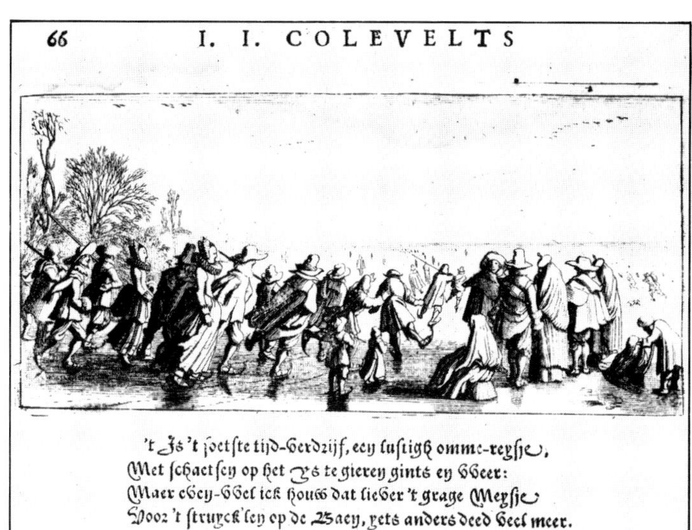

't Is 't soetste tijd-verdrijf, een lustigh omme-reysje,
Met schaetsen op het Ys te gieren gints en weer:
Maer evenwel ick houde dat liever 't grage Meysje
Voor 't struyck'len op de Baey, yets anders deed veel meer.

Cat. #43

XXIV

Het mist een Meester wel.

HEt is niet nieuws inde plaetsen daer men ghewoon is Schaetsen te ghebruycken, dat een Man valt, soo hy de moet heeft dat hy weder op staet, en gaet zijn gangh oft niet gheschiedt en waer: daer men mede te verstaen wil gheven, dat niemand haeft om een kleyn ongheval den moet verliesen sal, het zy in zijn Rijckdom, in zijn Reeckeninghe, in zijn Ridderlijcke daden, in zijn Amoreusheden: dan moet met den Alchimist dencken, noch eens sal ick dat gaen beghinnen, per avontuere sal't dan wel zijn gheraeckt: ende soo het weder den selven gangh gaet, moet men de plaetse veranderen ende soecken onbekende lieden, daer de klocken een andere klanck gheven.

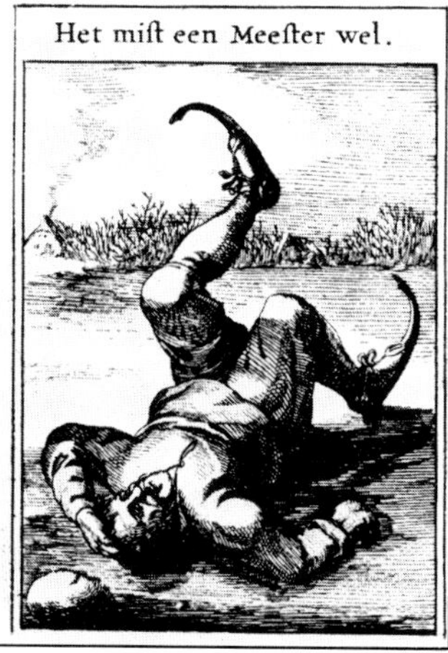

Cat. #45

VII

Ghoeffent derf.

SENECA schrijft in zijn Brieven, *Quem in ipsa re trepidare volueris, ante rem exerceas.*

Dat is:

Die ghy in eenige dingen wilt seecker ende vast doen gaen/ die moet ghy daer in oeffenen eer't in't werck komt.

Ghelijck het ryden op schaetsen, dat is een glibberighe gladde gang: maer die't wel kan, het doet dapper wegh spoeden: en al hoe wel het licht om doen schijnt, soo isset nochtãs swaer voor die eerst begint te leeren: soo gheeft dit woordt te kennen, en raedt elck een, dat hy hem in tijdts moet begheven tot leeren, om in zijn ouderdom te gebruycken, en die de grondt van zijn professie niet en kan, die angt en hangt altijdt, en derf noch kan niet besluyten wat in een sake best ghedaen of gheseyt is.

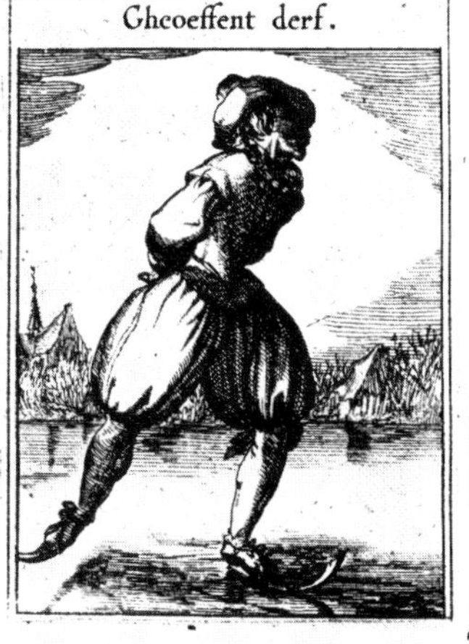

Cat. #44

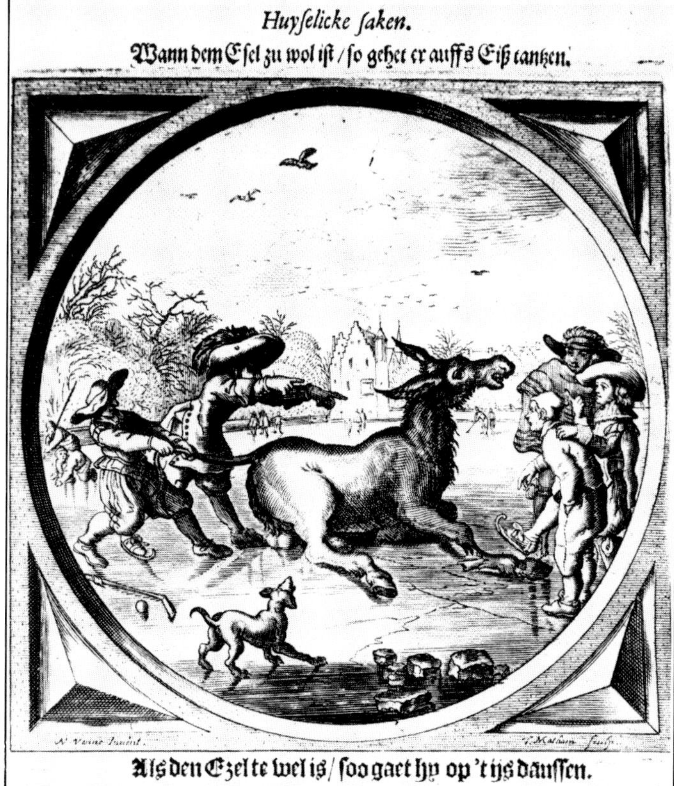

Cat. #46

SKATING AND FOLLY

A predictable, and more pleasant, aspect of ice skating was the humor associated with the sport. The skater's first time on the ice shared the scene with many indecorous tumbles in Dutch paintings and prints, some of which relate closely to the moralizing texts and pictures of emblem books. Hessel Gerritsz copied Visscher's emblem of the fallen man (Cat. #45), placing it squarely in the midst of a skating scene set before the Castle Zuylen (Cat. #48). Like the emblem after which it is modeled, the single-sheet engraving contains an explanatory text that mirrors the message of Visscher's poem. Likewise, artists enjoyed depicting animals in human guise on the ice (Fig. 8). One of the most humorous examples is Bruegel's *Monkeys on the Ice* (Cat. #49) where monkeys dressed like people poke fun at the pride and vanity of the human race. Even before Darwin suggested the concept of human evolution, the relationship between people and their simian cousins was unmistakable.

"The world goes on skates," a proverb that mirrored the instability and waywardness of life, is the subject of many humorous crowd scenes of skaters on ice. Bruegel's engraving entitled *Ice Scene Before the Gate of St. George, Antwerp* (Cat. #50) contains an inscription in three languages that alludes to the various ways in which people conduct their lives: "See how they skate at Antwerp, some going this way, some that; some stumble and fall while others walk proudly upright. Learn, then, from this picture, how we conduct ourselves in this world, wisely or foolishly, slipping and slithering our way through a life whose bases is even more ephemeral and fragile than ice."[32] Influenced by Bruegel's engraving, Bol's *Winter* (Cat. #51) and Hondius's *January* (Cat. #52) reflect the variety of human experience represented by every possible activity on the ice. A woman just learning to stand on skates is pushed along by three male

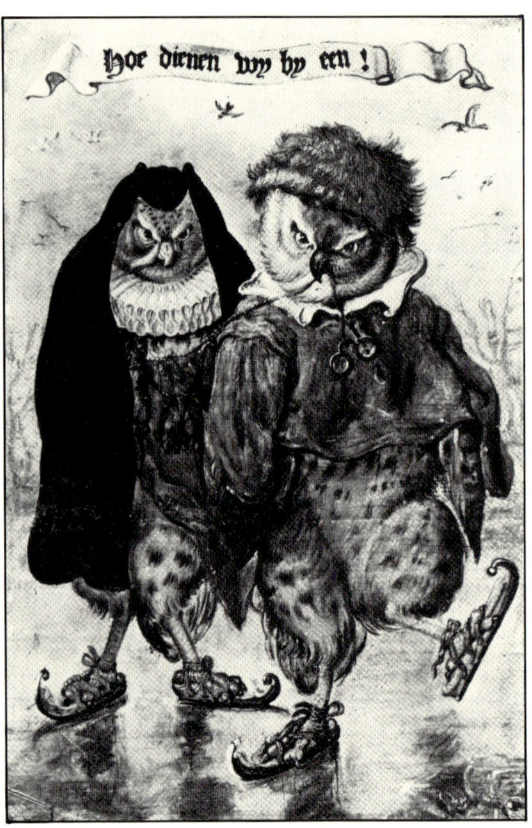

Figure 8 C. Bloemaert, *Owls on the Ice* (Rotterdam, Museum Boymans-van Beuningen)

helpers—an affectionate husband instructs his dutiful
wife—another couple falls indecorously—a man
struggles to raise himself above a hole in the ice—all
are objects for caricature and all mimic the vicissitudes
of life.

The delight that Bruegel took in illustrating the
pithy wisdom of proverbs and emblems can also be
discerned in his painting *Winter Landscape with Bird
Trap* (Cat. #1). A popular subject—over sixty versions
of this work exist—the painting depicts a gray winter
landscape teeming with skaters, hockey players,
children spinning tops—nearly every type of human
activity possible on ice. In the right foreground is a bird
trap, where dozens of unsuspecting birds cluster,
oblivious to the immediate danger that envelopes them.
Recent scholarship convincingly argues that this
painting is more than a depiction of simple reality and
that, like many of the works in this exhibition, it
expresses allegorical and moralizing ideas clothed in
everyday dress.[33]

Scenes of bird traps and fowling, like images of
skating, were common metaphors for the Christian
journey from inherited sin to salvation—beset all the
way by constant danger and temptation. Traditionally,
birds symbolized the human soul, and the fowler with
his traps, snares and nets represented the Devil. Satan
was perceived as lying in wait, like the birdcatcher, for
a human soul—a bird—to stray into his net. Hans
Sebald Beham illustrated the allegory in his print of a
monstrous devil/bird-catcher carrying an owl—a false
decoy—to lure the imprudent into his trap (Fig. 9).[34]
The Bible provided theological precedent for this
analogy. Psalms 124:7, for example, exalts: ''Our soul
is escaped as a bird out of the snare of the fowler: the
snare is broken and we are escaped.'' Psalm 10:7-8
declares that the devil ''...sitteth in the lurking places
of the villages: in the secret places doth he murder the
innocent...he lieth in wait to catch the poor: he doth
catch the poor, when he draweth him into his net.'' In
this context, Bruegel's *Winter Landscape with Bird
Trap* suggests that, like the simple bird that goes after
the fowler's bait and risks its life, the heedless person
who succumbs to temptation risks his immortal soul.
Bruegel's country skaters are heedless of the presence
of the Devil in everyday guise. They risk losing their
souls through the folly of misspent lives.

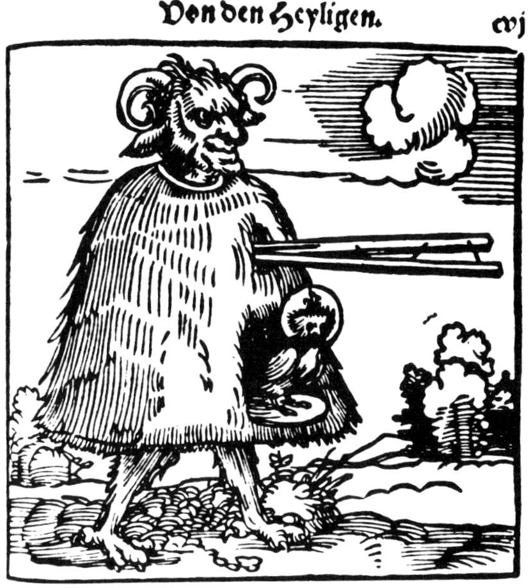

Figure 9 H. S. Beham, "The Devil
as Bird Catcher," from J. von
Schwarzenberg, *Die Beschwerung
der alten Teufelischen Schlangen...*,
Nurenberg, 1525, fol. CVI
(London, British Library)

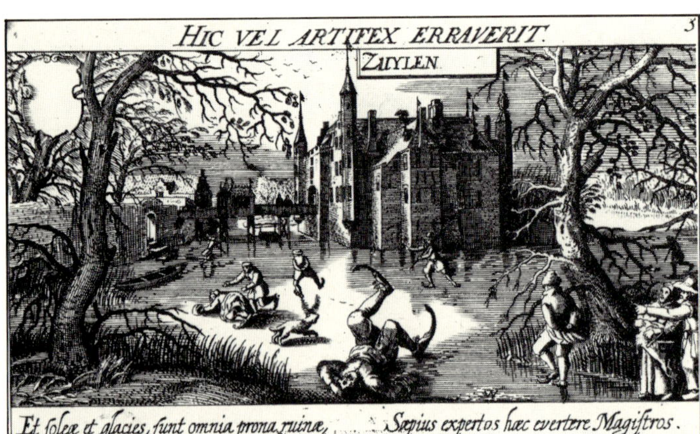

Cat. #48

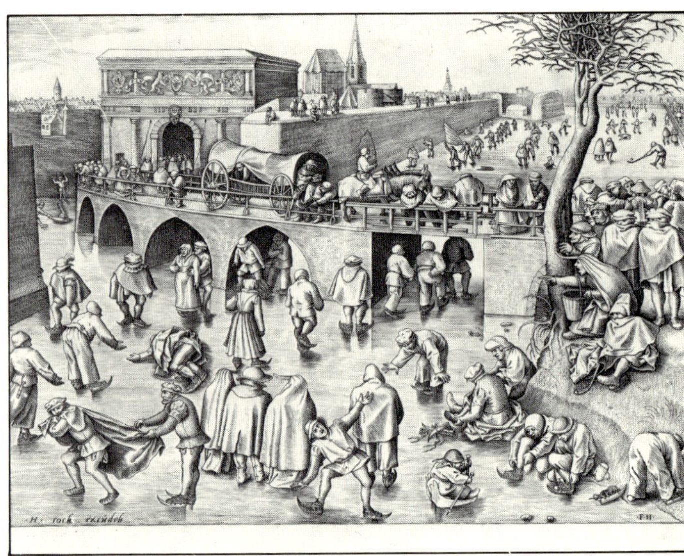

Cat. #50

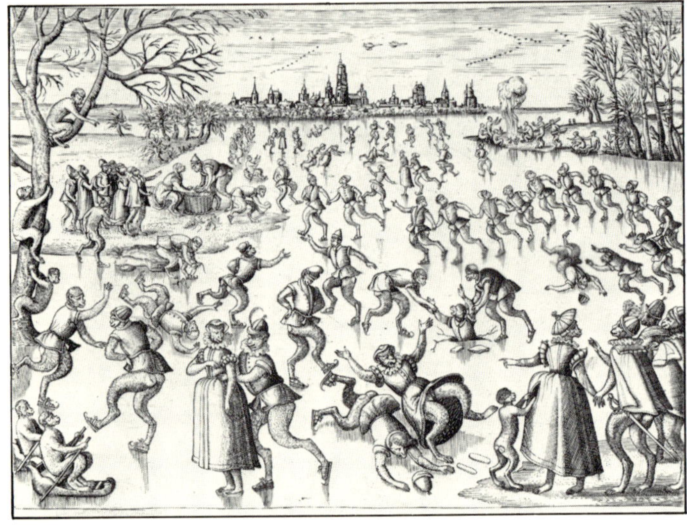

Cat.#49

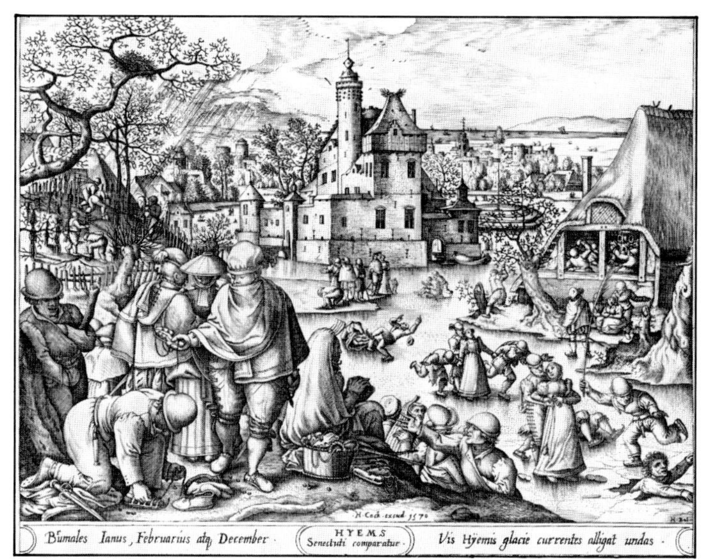

H. Cock excud. 1570
Bumales Ianus, Februarius atq; December.
HYEMS
Senectuti comparatur.
Vis Hyemis glacie currentes alligat undas.

Cat. #51

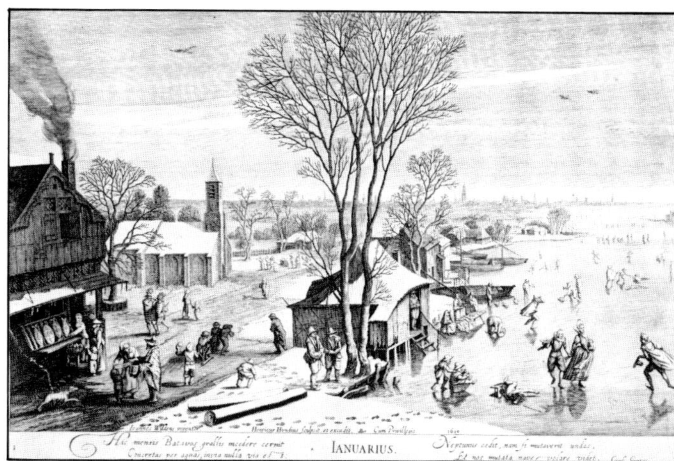

Ioannes Wildens inventor   Henricus Hondius sculpsit et excudit   Cum Privilegio   1614
Hic mensis Batavos grallis mecedere cernit   IANUARIUS.   Neptunus cedit, nam si mutaverit undas,
Concretas per aquas, meta nulla via est.   Et nos mutata nave volare videt.

Cat. #52

SKATING AND LOVE

The Dutch treated the topic of love with a ribald frankness some might label as coarse. It is wrong, however, to judge the 17th century by our own post-Victorian standards of morality. The Dutch were lenient toward male-female relationships and enjoyed poking fun at the folly of romance. Skating scenes offered just such an opportunity, often including a young woman who has just fallen on the ice and exposed herself in the process (Cat. #53). An attractive female might also be shown skating obliviously while the wind billows her skirts upward to the delight of the men on the shore. Such images offer conclusive proof that 17th century women had not yet discovered the advantages of wearing undergarments, even in cold weather.

Despite the possibility of public embarrassment, ice skating became a fashionable activity. The proverb, "Put on your skates even if you are a lady,"[35] attests to the widespread popularity of skating among women. Skating was good exercise, as "Ladies who imagine themselves incapable of walking two miles at a stretch, will skate miles without feeling fatigued...."[36] It is worth remembering that female "hysteria" was a common complaint among 17th century society maidens. Doctors prescribed mild outdoor exercise for the weakness and swooning that characterized this complaint. Skating was favored because it could be pursued at a relaxing pace, allowing the gentle regular movements of the legs to re-establish the natural rhythm of the body.[37]

Less liberated foreign chroniclers noted with amazement how well Dutch women took to the ice. During Cromwell's protectorate, when the English royal family was exiled to Holland, the French ambassador wrote that: "'Twas a very extraordinary thing to see the Princess of Orange clad in petticoats shorter than are generally worn by ladies so strictly decorous, these tucked up half-way to her waist, and with iron pattens on her feet learning to slide sometimes poised on one leg, sometimes on the other."[38] The graceful movements associated with ice skating were also perfected by Marie Antoinette of France, perhaps because, as Robert Jones's 18th century *Treatise on Skating* suggested: "No motion can be more happily imagined for setting off an elegant figure...."[39] Not all women feigned delicacy on skates, however. Travelers to the Low Countries were warned: "When skating in Holland, be careful how you show off your speed before a lady, or you may have the pleasure of following in her wake instead of being her leader."[40]

Images of ecstatic lovers gliding in perfect harmony over the ice attest to the popularity of skating as a favored mode of courtship (Fig. 10, Cat. #53, #54, #55). The inscription beneath van der Bremden's engraving after A. van de Venne (Fig. 10) implies that the warmth of love can make the harshness of winter easier to bear: "Horrible winter lies barren, but is made tolerable by the warmth of fire, when the sun raises its orb and flagrant torch." The emotion of love was understood as a warm sanguine passion, capable of mitigating the coldness of the phlegmatic temperament by opening the heart. Thus, doctors commonly prescribed "falling in love" for people suffering from an over-abundance of phlegm and melancholy.[41] For artists, pair skating, which involved touching, holding hands and moving in synchrony, was the perfect metaphor for favorable love.

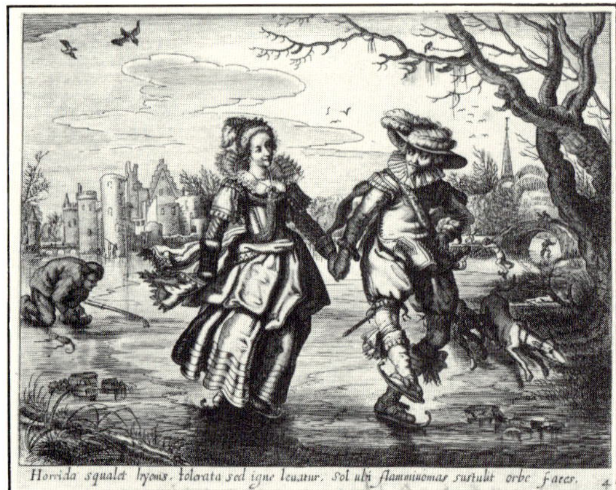

Figure 10 D. van der Bremden after A. van de Venne, *Winter*, etch., (Amsterdam, Rijksprentenkabinet #A16314)

The pragmatic Dutch knew, however, that harmony and happiness in love and life are fleeting and unpredictable. Some of the lovers on skates do not notice the large crack that has formed beneath them. Others skate, rapturously looking into each others' eyes, straight toward a nasty tree stump that looms in their path. Moreover, ice skating offered the same opportunities for adulterous love as it did for innocent courtship. Robert Jones, who wrote the first "how-to" book on skating in the 18th century, listed among the advantages of the sport the fact that "A lady may indulge herself in a tête-à-tête with an acquaintance without provoking the jealousy of her husband."[42]

Artists employed the skating metaphor to signify both the difficulties and the raptures of love. Hondius's engraving after Matthias Bril (Cat. #56) illustrates such a scene, showing a well-dressed couple expertly negotiating the ice while the female half of another couple has just fallen behind them, indecorously exposing her rump to her partner. The two skating pairs within the same picture represent harmonious and inharmonious love. An illustration from Jacob Cats's moralistic book, s'Weerelts begin…" (Cat. #57), implies that disaster in love is like an accident on the ice. The image shows a young man and women who have fallen through a hole and are offered a ladder by friends on the shore. A more subtle allegory of love's wayward fortunes appears in H. van der Burgh's painting entitled *The Terrace* (Fig. 11). Here, two lovers stand together in a warm springtime garden, complete with all the attributes of Venus—musical instruments, wine, flowers and little stone cupids poised on the garden railing. On closer inspection, however, one of the cupids is seen to be wearing ice skates. Though the sun shines and flowers bloom in the garden, the naked cupid shivers with cold. Placed near the center of the picture, he clearly points to the possibility of adversity in love, even within the idyllic garden of Venus. Love, like luck, is shown to be unpredictable.

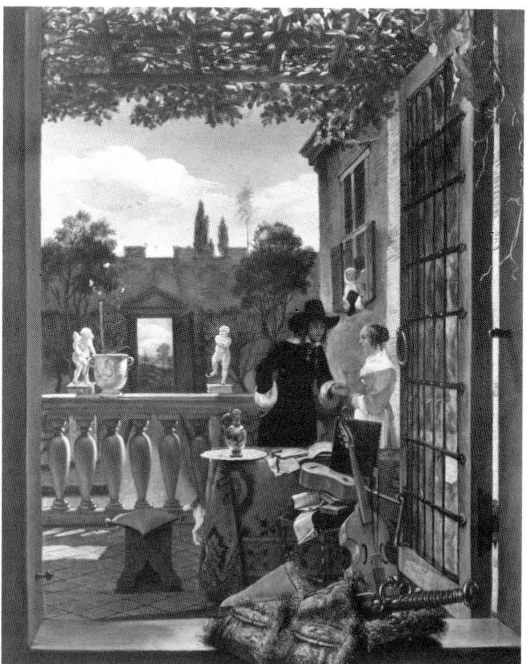

Figure 11 H. van der Burgh, *The Terrace***, oil (Chicago, Art Institute)**

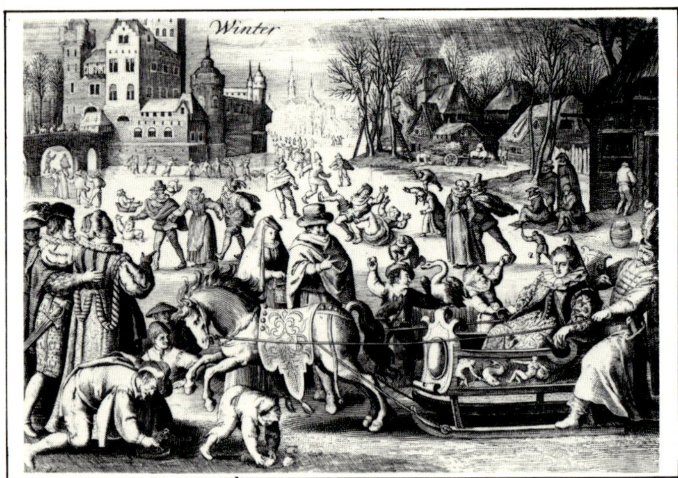
Winter

Cat. #53

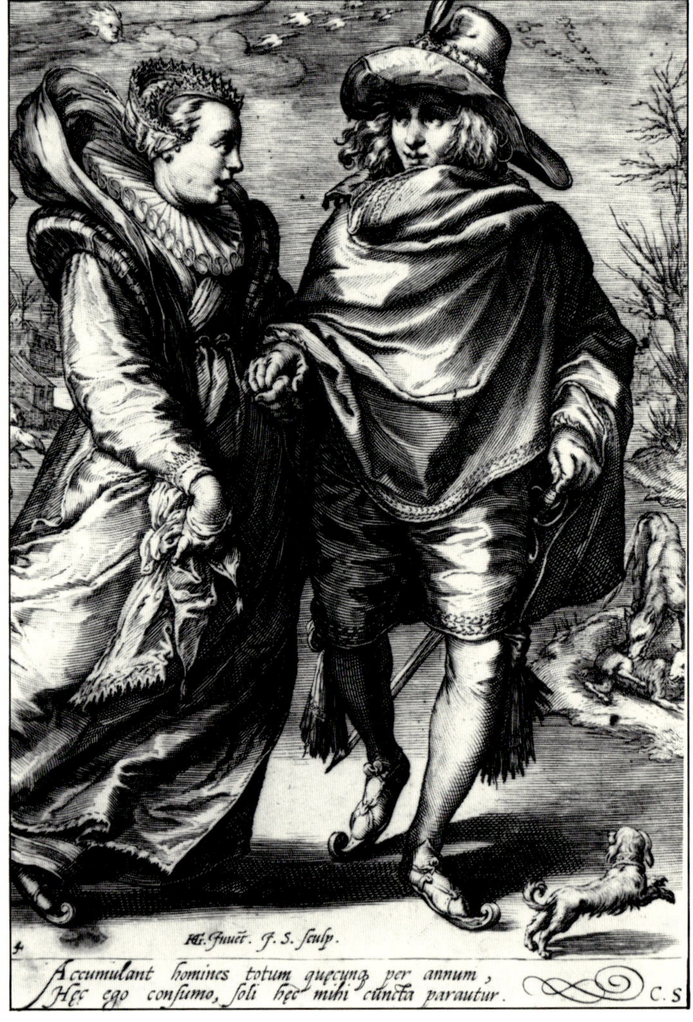
Hi. Guuer. G. S. sculp.
Accumulant homines totum quęcunq per annum,
Hęc ego consumo, soli hęc mihi cuncta parautur.
C. S

Cat. #54

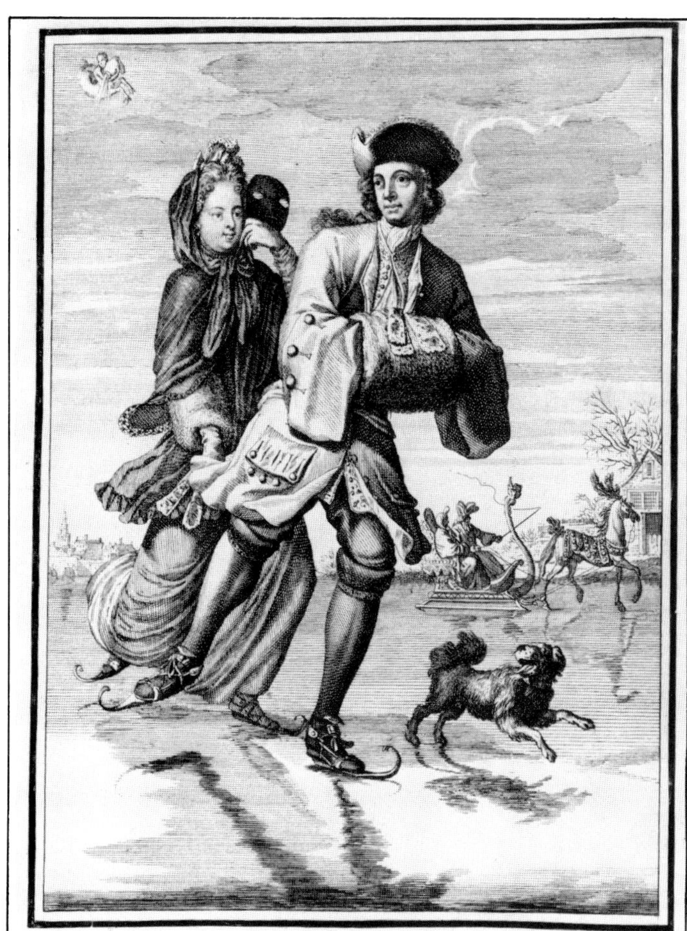

Cat. #55

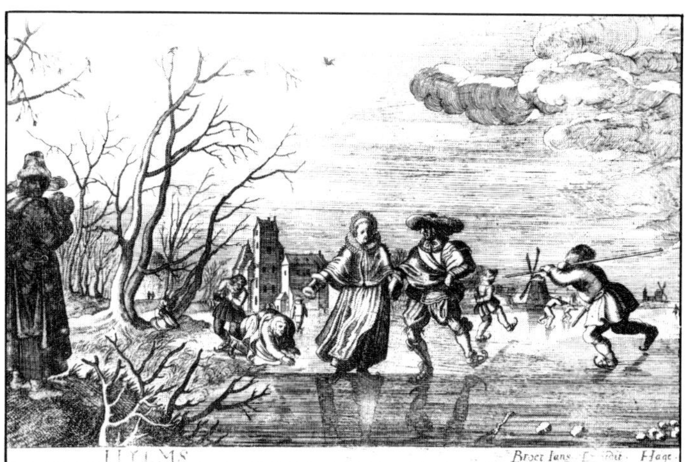

Cat. #56

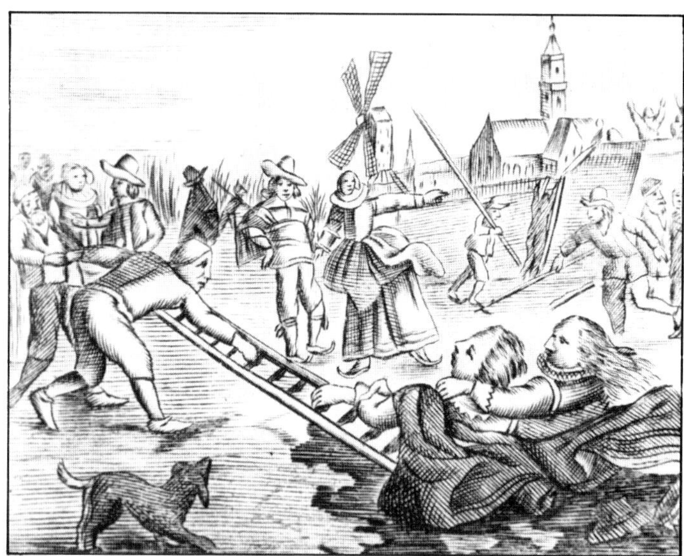

Cat. #57

The Dutch Tradition in America

The British introduced ice skating to this country, having learned it from the Dutch. The Northeastern U.S.A., which retained its harsh winters and frozen lakes even after the little ice age ended in Europe, was the ideal place for the continued development of the sport. The modern art of skating, which is practiced today for fun and profit worldwide, has its roots in the Dutch solution to the practical problems of negotiating their frozen waterways.

American figure skating seems to have begun in Philadelphia, where it was introduced by English soldiers during the Revolutionary War. John Adams's letter to his son, written in 1780, advises taking up the British sport for both health and pleasure: "I have seen some Officers of the British Army, at Boston, and some of the Army at Cambridge, skait with perfect Elegance, as if they had spent their whole lives in the study of Holgarths Principles of Beauty, and in reducing them to Practice."[43] For a hundred years after the Revolution, Philadelphia remained the only place in America where figure skating was taken seriously. The Bushnell all-steel clamp-on skate was invented there in 1848. Though it bore the expensive price tag of $30, the skate revolutionized the sport, allowing skaters to spin and leap without throwing their blades. Members of the Philadelphia Skating and Humane Society, formed in 1849, were concerned not only with practicing their moves and figures, but also with rescuing skaters who broke through the ice of the dangerous Schuylkill River. Like similar early Dutch organizations, the Philadelphia Society was a privileged group dedicated to civic harmony and protection.[44] Like the first American skaters, early American artists derived their craft from what they remembered of English painting, which, during 17th and 18th centuries, was dominated by an imported Dutch tradition. The technical advances of the 19th century allowed illustrators like Currier & Ives to mass-produce images of "Americana" such as *Central Park, Winter, The Skating Pond* (Cat. #58). Currier & Ives's cross section of American society corresponds to Bruegel's *Ice Scene Before the Gate of St. George, Antwerp* (Cat. #50)— some folk skate in pairs, some fall, others are just learning to stand on ice. Thomas Birch's *Skating* (Cat. #59), like its Dutch prototypes, places ice skating within the larger context of a winter landscape. Here, skaters play on a frozen country pond, an image framed by bare winter trees reminiscent of the organization of van der Neer's *Winter Landscape* (Cat. #2). Though the moralistic tone of Dutch art is missing from the American works, the universal appeal of skating comes through in both traditions. The allegorical link of skating with danger and death, however, was not lost on artist Hugo Simberg. His *Death on Skates* (c. 1917) (Cat. #60) reflects the same macabre fascination with fate that van Rusting's *Death and the Skaters* (Cat. #36) did in the 17th century. Clearly, Simberg's link of ice skating with the larger human concerns of life and death owes much to the Dutch moralizing tradition.

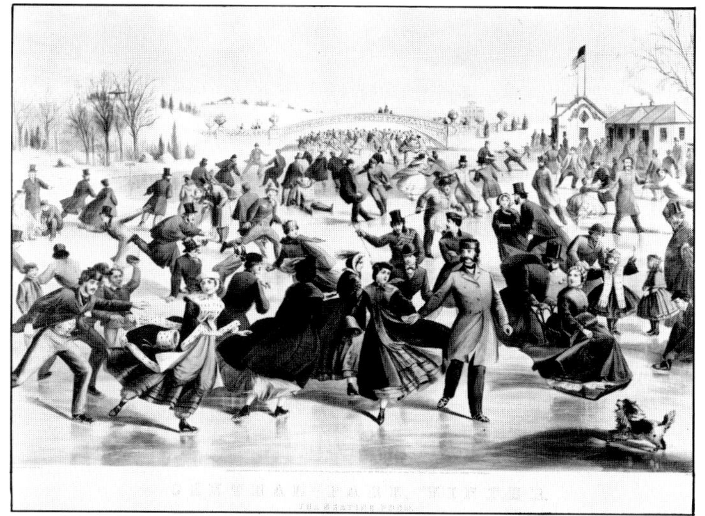

Cat. #58

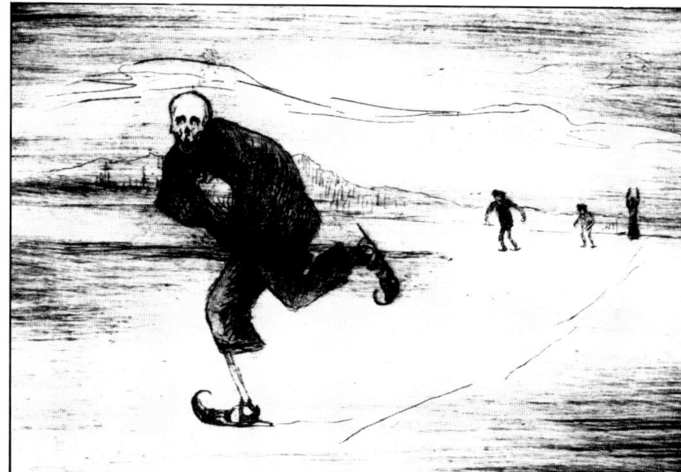

Cat. #60

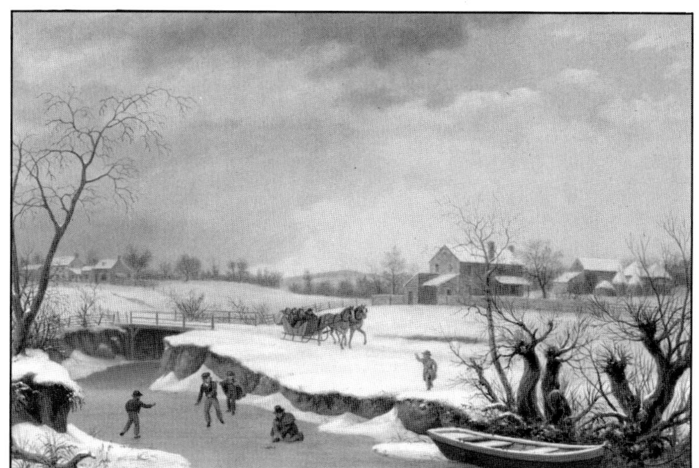

Cat. #59

Epilogue

Ironically, the pinnacle of ice skating's popularity coincided with the end of the little ice age in Europe. Means had to be found to continue the sport that had evolved during four centuries into a nearly universal activity. As early as 1760, London musical instrument maker Joseph Merlin devised a pair of skates on wheels.[45] "Roller skating," as it was called, thus began as a substitute for ice skating. Another solution to the problem of lack of natural ice was to devise an alternative surface for skating. The first artificial rink of this type was produced in 1842 by Henry Kirk of England. Its surface consisted of a hard, slippery mixture of crystallized alum mixed with hogs' grease, salts of soda and melted sulfur. Kirk set up his "miniature alpine lake," measuring 50′ x 70′, in London's Baker Street. The experiment was doomed, however, for the synthetic ice smelled awful and was soon too cut up to skate upon. Clearly, the ideal surface for skating was still frozen water, and the only solution to the problem was to produce ice by artificial means. This first happened in 1870, when Matthew Bujac of New York created ice by circulating ammonia gas through tubes placed beneath the water's surface.[46] The first patented ice rinks appeared a few years later in England, where surface water was chilled by glycerin flowing through copper pipes.[47] These indoor rinks allowed skating during the entire year and led to a rapid improvement in skating technique.

The first World Championship skating competition was held in 1896, and skating's recognition as an Olympic sport began in 1908.[48] Competitive skating was, however, formalized as early as the 18th century. The first official "skating club" was begun in Edinburgh, at about the same time that Robert Jones, another Scot, wrote his *Treatise on Skating*. The Edinburgh Skating Club set high standards of expertise, requiring prospective members to "skate a complete circle on each foot and jump over first one, then two, then three hats."[49] Members were restricted to men only, who wore the prescribed white tie, tails and tall hat while skating. Though juvenile by today's super-athletes' standards, the entrance requirements required by the Edinburgh club began the art of competitive figure skating.

The history of skating since the 18th century is filled with illustrious names of skaters too numerous to mention. Among the many who revolutionized the art of skating are: Jackson Haynes, who was the first to add music to his routine in 1860; Ulrich Salchow, winner of the first Olympic skating competition, ten world championships and inventor of the Salchow jump; Madge Syers-Cave, the first woman to distinguish herself in a world championship and to establish recognition of women as equals of men in technique; Sonja Henie, who, as a child of eleven, astonished the world at the Olympic Games of 1924 and thereafter entered the Hollywood celebrity mainstream; Dick Button, whose phenomenal leaps won him five successive world championships from 1948-1952; Ludmilla Belousova and Oleg Protopopov, whose balletic grace and athletic excellence revolutionized pair skating—the roster of great skaters becomes longer each year. Lydwine of Schiedam, patron saint of skaters (Cat. #34), is undoubtedly relieved that her martyrdom on the ice was not in vain.

Notes

**SKATING IN THE ARTS OF
17ᵗʰ CENTURY HOLLAND**
1. See W. Stechow, *Dutch Landscape Painting of the Seventeenth Century*, London & New York, 1966
2. See L. G. Stevenson, "'New Diseases' in the 17th Century," *Bulletin of the History of Medicine*, Jan.-Feb., 1965, XXXIX, 1-21
3. See J. A. Mazzeo, Ed., *Reason and Imagination—Studies in the History of Ideas 1600-1800*, New York/London, 1962

THE HISTORY OF ICE SKATING
4. M. Heller, Ed., *The Illustrated Encyclopedia of Ice Skating*, New York, 1979
5. I. Brokow, *The Art of Skating*, New York, 1926, p.6
6. *Ibid.*, p.2
7. *Ibid.*, p.7
8. J. M. Heathcote & C. G. Tebbutt, *Skating*, London, 1892, p.7
9. E. van Straaten, *Koud tot op het Bot*, s'Gravenhage, 1977, p.10
10. Heller, as in note #4
11. A. M. Meijerman, *Hollandse Winters*, Antwerp, 1967, p.88
The Early Art of Skating
12. Heller, as in note #4
13. Brokow, as in note 5, p.13
14. Heller, as in note #4, p. 203
15. *Ibid.*
16. Meijerman, as in note 11, p. 54
17. *Skating*, January, 1973, pp.14-15
Games on the Ice
18. R. Flower, *The Story of Skiing and Other Winter Sports*, London, 1976, p. 12
19. Heathcote & Tebbutt, as in note #8, p. 246
20. Heller, as in note #4, pp. 201-208
The National Sport of Holland
21. For a discussion of Holland's government in the 17th century, see: C. Wilson, *The Dutch Republic and the Civilization of the Seventeenth Century*, New York/Toronto, 1977

SKATING AS ALLEGORY
22. Meijerman, as in note 11, pp. 88-90; see also D. Bax, *Hieronymus Bosch...*, Rotterdam, 1979, p. 18
23. L. Stone-Ferrier, *Dutch Prints of Daily Life*, Lawrence, Kansas, 1983, p. 158.
24. For alchemical imagery in Bosch's *St. Anthony* triptych, see: L. Dixon, "Bosch's *St. Anthony* Triptych: An Apothecary's Apotheosis,' *Art Journal*, 44, 1984, pp. 119-132
Winter
25. See: B. L. Gordon, *Medieval and Renaissance Medicine*, New York, 1959

26. The system of humours and elements was part of ancient Greek Hippocratic medical tradition. See: B. Farrington, *Greek Science*, London, 1961. For a discussion of humoral theory in the works of a Dutch 16th century artist, see: I. M. Veldman, "Seasons, Planets and Temperaments in the Work of Maarten van Heemskerck...," *Simiolus*, XI, 1980
Skating Emblems
27. L. Réau, *Iconographie de l'art Chrétien*, III, Paris, 1958, pp. 842-843
28. Brokow, as in note 5, p. 3
29. Meijerman, as in note 11, p. 51
30. For discussions of the ambiguity between emblem and work of art, see: P. Sutton, *Masters of 17th-century Dutch Genre Painting*, Philadelphia, 1984, pp. xxi-xxv; and Stone-Ferrier, as in note 23, p. 103
31. Dutch art historian E. de Jongh pioneered the study of the relationship of 17th-century Dutch art to emblem literature. See particularly E. de Jongh, *Tot lering en vermaak*, Amsterdam, 1974
Skating and Folly
32. See: A. Monballieu; "P. Bruegel's *Schaatsenrijden bij de St.-Jorispoort te Antwerpen...*," *Jaarboek van het koninklijk Museum voor schone Kunsten Antwerpen*, 1981, pp. 17-29.
33. L. Bauer & G. Bauer, "The *Winter Landscape with Skaters and Bird Trap* by Pieter Bruegel the Elder," *Art Bulletin*, LXVI, 1984, pp. 145-150.
34. For the early Northern tradition of depicting Satan as entrapper, see: M. Schapiro, "'Muscipula Diaboli,' The Symbolism of the *Merode Altarpiece*," *Art Bulletin*, XXVII, 1945, pp. 182-187.
Skating and Love
35. Heathcote & Tebbutt, as in note 8, p. 224
36. *Ibid.*, p. 190
37. See: I. Veith, *Hysteria, the History of a Disease*, Chicago, 1965
38. Flower, as in note 18, p. 15
39. *Ibid.*, p. 18
40. Heathcote & Tebbutt, as in note 8, p. 230
41. Veith, as in note 37
42. Flower, as in note 18, p. 18

THE DUTCH TRADITION IN AMERICA
43. Quoted in R. Sheffield & R. Woodward, *The Ice Skating Book*, New York, n.d., p. 32
44. *Ibid.*

EPILOGUE
45. Heathcote & Tebbutt, as in note 8, p. 11
46. *Ibid.*, pp. 14-15
47. Brokow, as in note 5, p. 7
48. *Ibid.*, p. 9
49. *Ibid.*, p. 5

SUGGESTED READINGS
Life in 17th-Century Holland
T. Aston, ed., *Crisis in Europe 1560-1660—Essays from Past and Present*, London, 1965

K.H.D. Haley, *The Dutch in the 17th Century*, London, 1972

J. H. Huizinga, *Dutch Civilization in the 17th Century*, trans. A. J. Pomerans, London, 1968

J. A. Mazzeo, ed., *Reason and Imagination—Studies in the History of Ideas 1600-1800*, New York/London, 1962

C. Wilson, *The Dutch Republic and the Civilization of the Seventeenth Century*, New York/Toronto, 1977

P. Zumthor, *Daily Life in Rembrandt's Holland*, New York, 1963

Dutch Art—General Surveys
S. Alpers, *The Art of Describing: Dutch Art of the 17th Century*, Chicago, 1983

C. Brown, *Art in the 17th Century*, London, 1976

C. Bugler, *Dutch Painting in the 17th Century*, New York, 1979

H. Guratzsch, *Painting in the Low Countries*, London, 1981

F.W.H. Hollstein, *Dutch and Flemish Etchings, Engravings, and Woodcuts, ca. 1450-1700*, Vols. 1—, Amsterdam, 1949—

W. Martin, trans. B. Harning, *Dutch Painting of the Great Period*, London/New York, 1951

J. Rosenberg & S. Slive, *Dutch Art & Architecture, 1600-1800*, Baltimore, 1966

W. Stechow, *Dutch Landscape Painting in the 17th Century*, New York, 1966

L. Stone-Ferrier, *Dutch Prints of Daily Life*, exhibition catalogue, Lawrence, Kansas, 1983

P. Sutton, *Masters of 17th Century Dutch Genre Painting*, exhibition catalogue, Philadelphia, 1984

Illustrated Histories of Skating
I. Brokow, *The Art of Skating*, New York, 1926

N. Brown, *Ice Skating: A History*, London, 1959

M. Cereghini, *5,000 Years of Winter Sports*, Milan, 1955

J. C. Dier, ed., *The Book of Winter Sports*, London, 1912

Der Eislauf in Kunst und Kulturgeschichte (Catalogue of the Gillis Grafstrom Collection, now housed at the United States Figure Skating Association, Colorado Springs), Hamburg, 1966

R. Flower, *The Story of Skiing and Other Winter Sports*, London, 1976

M. Hardie, "The Pictorial History of Skating—A Suggestion for Collectors," *Connoisseur*, March, 1906, XIV, pp. 151-157

J. M. Heathcote & C. G. Tebbutt, *Skating*, London, 1892

M. Heller, ed., *The Illustrated Encyclopedia of Ice Skating*, New York, 1979

The Hood Museum of Art, Dartmouth College, *Winter*, exhibition catalogue, Hanover, New Hampshire, 1985

A. M. Meijerman, *Hollandse Winters*, Antwerp, 1967

The Munson Williams Proctor Institute, *The Olympics in Art*, exhibition catalogue, Utica, New York, 1980

R. Sheffield & R. Woodward, *The Ice Skating Book*, New York, n.d.

E. van Straaten, *Koud tot op het Bot*, 's-Gravenhage, 1977

CATALOGUE OF THE EXHIBITION:

Cat. #1: School of Pieter Bruegel the Elder, *Winter Landscape with Bird Trap*, c. 1560, oil on panel, 15″ h. x 22″ w., collection of Frederick and Jan Mayer.

Cat. #2: Aert van der Neer, *Winter Landscape*, c. 1650, oil on canvas, 23″ h. x 27½″ w., Cincinnati Art Museum, OH; gift of Audrey Emery.

Cat. #3: Barent Avercamp, *Games on the Ice*, 1654, oil on panel, 10¾″ h. x 17⁷⁄₁₆″ w., High Museum of Art, Atlanta, GA; gift of Rolf R. Roland.

Cat. #4: F. Reinzer, *Meteorologi philosophico-politica…*, 1709, Augustae Vindelichorum, p. 144, emblem book, The Library of Congress, Washington, DC

Cat. #5: Anonymous, *Ysgezigt op de Lagune van Venetie*, 1708, engraving, 4⅝″ h. x 6¹¹⁄₁₆″ h., the United States Figure Skating Association (USFSA), World Figure Skating Hall of Fame and Museum, Colorado Springs, CO; Gillis Grafstrom Collection.

Cat. #6: Cornelis Visscher after Cornelis Claesz, *Skaters near a Shipyard*, n.d., engraving, 5½″ h. x 7½″ w., USFSA; Gillis Grafstrom Collection.

Cat. #7: Cornelis Visscher after Adrian van Ostade, *Der Schaatsenrijder*, n.d., engraving, 16¾″ h. x 13⅜″ w., USFSA; Gillis Grafstrom Collection.

Cat. #8: Olaus Magnus, *Historia de Gentium Septentrionalium…*, Basel, 1567, emblem book, The New York Public Library, NY, NY; Rare Books and Manuscripts Division.

Cat. #9: Anonymous, *Types of Footware*, 16th century, engraving, 11⁷⁄₃₂″ h. x 11¹³⁄₁₆″ w., USFSA; Gillis Grafstrom Collection.

Cat. #10: Abraham and Frederik Bloemaert, *Youth Tying on Skates*, c. 1630, engraving, 7½″ h. x 5²⁵⁄₃₂″ w., USFSA; Gillis Grafstrom Collection.

Cat. #11: Examples of old skates:
  a. Strap-on Skate with curled prow, acorn embellishment, n.d., wood, metal, and leather, 11³¹⁄₃₂″ long.
  b. 17″ Racing Skate, n.d., wood and metal, 17″ long.
  c. Child's Skate with tight curled prow, n.d., wood and metal, 10¹³⁄₁₆″ long.
  d. "Mudwalkers," n.d., wood, leather, and metal, 4¹⁷⁄₃₂″, 6²⁷⁄₃₂″, and 9⅝″ long.
USFSA; Gillis Grafstrom Collection.

Cat. #12: Jan van Goyen, *Country Folk on the Ice*, c. 1650, sepia and pen wash drawing on paper, 7¼″ h. x 6⅛″ w., USFSA; Gillis Grafstrom Collection.

Cat. #13: Jacob Gole after Cornelis Dusart, *December* (from the *Twelve Months*), n.d., mezzotint, 8½″ h. x 6″ w. platemark, Museum of Fine Arts, Boston, MA; Harvey D. Parker Collection.

Cat #14: Anonymous, Delft titles (8), including pair skating and boys with poles, n.d., glazed ceramic, collection of Mr. Dick Button.

Cat. #15: C. Weigel, *Ethica Natuualis seu documenta moralia*, plate #51, 1700, emblem book, the New York Public Library, NY, NY; General Research Division.

Cat. #16: Will Warter, publisher, *Great Ice Feast on the Thames in the Unusually Cold Winter of 1683*, n.d., engraving, 13⅜″ h. x 16⅛″ w., USFSA; Gillis Grafstrom Collection.

Cat. #17: Anton von Prenner, *Hocke Pinx*, n.d., engraving, collection of Mr. Dick Button.

Cat. #18: Henricus Hondius after Broer Janssen, *Curling on the Ice*, n.d., engraving, 6³⁄₁₆″ h. x 10¼″ w., USFSA; Gillis Grafstrom Collection.

Cat. #19: Pieter van der Borcht after B. de Momper, *Grote Schaatsfeest te Mechelen*, 1559, etching, 11¼″ h. x 18½″ w. sheet, Museum of Fine Arts, Boston, MA; Katherine E. Bullard Fund in Memory of Francis Bullard.

Cat. #20: P. Nolpe after Pieter Potter, *Der Winter*, 1650, engraving, 12⅛″ h. x 20¹⁄₁₆″ w., USFSA; Gillis Grafstrom Collection.

Cat. #21: Frisius after D. Vinckboons, *Hyems (The Winter)*, n.d., the New York Public Library; Prints Collection.

Cat. #22: Pieter Bout, *Winter Scene*, n.d., etching, 10½″ h. x 7½″ w., Museum of Fine Arts, Boston, MA; Harvey D. Parker Collection.

Cat. #23: Pieter Quast, *Peasant*, c. 1630, engraving, 8¼″ h. x 6¹¹⁄₃₂″ w., USFSA; Gillis Grafstrom Collection.

Cat. #24: Simon Fokker after Hendrick Avercamp, *Buiten Alkmaar*, c. 1619, engraving, 7″ h. x 10¼″ w., USFSA; Gillis Grafstrom Collection.

Cat. #25: J. Moligns, "Antwerp" from *Die Nieuwe Chronijke van Brabant*, Antwerp, 1565, the New York Public Library, NY; Rare Books and Manuscripts Division.

Cat. #26: Reiner Nooms (called Zeeman), *The Blockhouses, Amsterdam*, n.d., etching, 10¹¹⁄₁₆″ h. x 6⁹⁄₁₆″ w., USFSA; Gillis Grafstrom Collection.

Cat. #27: Hessel Gerritsz after D. Vinckboons, *Winter: Castle Slot Zuijlen* (from the series, *The Seasons: View of Castles in the Vicinity of Amsterdam*), n.d., etching, 7⅞″ h. x 10⅝″ w. sheet, Hood Museum of Art, Dartmouth College, Hanover, NH.

Cat. #28: Jan van der Velde II, *January*, n.d., etching, 10¹⁵⁄₁₆″ h. x 14½″ w., the National Gallery of Art, Washington, DC; Rosenwald Collection.

Cat. #29: J. Barre after P. Stevens, *Winter*, c. 1689, engraving, the Metropolitan Museum of Art, NY, NY; The Elisha Whittelsey Fund, 1949.

Cat. #30: Crispijn de Passe the Elder after Maarten de Vos, *January*, n.d., 16″ h. x 22″ w. matted, Cincinnati Art Museum, OH.

Cat. #31: J. Sadeler after D. Barendsz, *Winter*, n.d., engraving, 6⅞″ h. x 8⅞″ w., the Metropolitan Museum of Art, NY, NY; The Elisha Whittelsey Fund, 1949.

Cat. #32: J. Sadeler after H. Bol, *Winter*, 1580, engraving, the Metropolitan Museum of Art; Harris Brisbane Dick Fund, 1953.

Cat. #33: J. Collaert after J. de Momper, *February*, n.d., engraving, the Metropolitan Museum of Art, NY, NY; Harris Brisbane Dick Fund.

Cat. #34: "The Martyrdom of St. Lydvine" from Johannes Brugman, *Vita Lydvinae*, Schiedam, 1498, the Pierpont Morgan Library, NY, NY.

Cat. #35: "The Skatemaker" from J. and C. Luiken, *Spiegel van het Manselijk Bedrijf*, Amsterdam, 1704, engraving, 8″ h. x 5½″ w. sheet; the Rare Book and Manuscript Library, Butler Library, Columbia University, NY, NY.

Cat. #36: "Death and the Skaters" from Salomon van Rusting, *Het Schouw-Toneel des Doods…*, Amsterdam, 1707, emblem book, the New York Public Library, NY, NY; General Research Division.

Cat. #37: "De boom der zonde in" in J. David, *Christeliicke Waerseggher…*, Antwerp, 1602, emblem book, Princeton University Library, Princeton, NJ.

Cat. #38: "Pedetentim" in G. Rollenhagius, *Selectorum emblematum centuria secunda*, Utrecht, 1613, emblem book, the Folger Shakespeare Library, Washington, DC

Cat. #39: Emblem XIX in Theodore de Bèze, *Icones…*, Geneva, 1580, emblem book, the New York Public Library, NY, NY; Rare Books and Manuscripts Division.

Cat. #40: "Frigore consistunt densata" in N. Taurellus, *Emblemata psychico-ethica…*, Nurenberg, 1602, emblem book, the Folger Shakespeare Library, Washington, DC

Cat. #41: G. Strauch, "Man Fallen on the Ice" and "A Man on Stilts," German Emblems, n.d., engravings, 7⅞″ h. x 6¹¹⁄₁₆″ w. and 7½″ h. x 6⁹⁄₃₂″ w., USFSA; Gillis Grafstrom Collection.

Cat. #42: "The Old Wife" in J. Cats, *Houwelick…*, Haerlem, 1642, emblem book, the New York Public Library, NY, NY; General Research Division.

Cat. #43: "Cupidos Dartslheydt" in anonymous, *Amsterdamsche Pegasus…*, Amsterdam, 1627, song book, the Library of Congress, Washington, DC

Cat. #44 and #45: Emblems VII and XXIV from Roemer Visscher, *Sinnepoppen*, Amsterdam, 1614, emblem book, the Newberry Library, Chicago, IL.

Cat. #46: "Huyselicke saken" in J. Cats, *Spiegel van den ouden en nieuwen tijt*, Amsterdam, 1632, emblem book, the Newberry Library, Chicago, IL.

Cat. #47: "Fide et Diffide" in Joachim Camerarius, *Symbolorum et Emblematicum ex Animalibus Quadrupedibus…*, Nurenberg, 1595 (bound with *Symbolorum et Emblematum ex re Herbavia*), emblem book, the New York Public Library, NY, NY; Rare Books and Manuscripts Division.

Cat. #48: Hessel Gerritsz, *Hic Vel Artifex Erravert*, 1630, engraving, 4⁷⁄₃₂″ h. x 5²⁹⁄₃₂″ w., USFSA; Gillis Grafstrom Collection.

Cat. #49: Pieter van der Borcht after Bruegel the Elder, *Monkeys on the Ice* (from *Le Jeu des Singes*), n.d., engraving, 8¾″ h. x 11¾″ w. platemark, Museum of Fine Arts, Boston, MA; Horatio Greenough Curtis Fund.

Cat. #50: Frans Huys after Bruegel the Elder, *Ice Scene Before the Gate of St. George, Antwerp*, n.d., engraving, 10½″ h. x 15″ w., Museum of Fine Arts, Boston, MA; Stephen Bullard Memorial Fund.

Cat. #51: Pieter van der Heyden after H. Bol, *Winter*, engraving, n.d., 8¹⁵⁄₁₆″ h. x 11⁵⁄₁₆″ w., the National Gallery of Art, Washington, DC; Rosenwald Collection.

Cat. #52: Henricus Hondius, *January*, 1624, engraving, collection of Mr. Dick Button.

Cat. #53: N. de Bruijn after Maarten de Vos, *Winter*, c. 1600, engraving, 7⅜″ h. x 11¹³⁄₃₂″ w., USFSA; Gillis Grafstrom Collection.

Cat. #54: Saenredam after Goltzius, *Winter*, n.d., engraving, 8²¹⁄₃₂″ h. x 6⁷⁄₃₂″ w., USFSA; Gillis Grafstrom Collection.

Cat. #55: C. Weigel after C. Luijken, *January*, c. 1700, engraving, 9²⁷⁄₃₂″ h. x 7⅛″ w., USFSA; Gillis Grafstrom Collection.

Cat. #56: Hendrick Hondius after Matthias Bril, *Pairs of Lovers*, c. 1620, engraving, 7¹¹⁄₃₂″ h. x 11¹³⁄₃₂″ w., USFSA; Gillis Grafstrom Collection.

Cat. #57: "Accident on the Ice" in J. Cats, *s'Weerelts begin, midden, eijinde besloten in den trouringh…*, Amsterdam, 1663, emblem book, Princeton University Library, Princeton, NJ.

Cat. #58: Currier & Ives, *Central Park, Winter, The Skating Pond*, n.d., colored lithograph, 22″ h. x 29″ w. sheet, the New York Public Library, NY, NY; Prints Collection.

Cat. #59: Thomas Birch, *Skating*, n.d., oil on canvas, 20″ h. x 30″ w., Museum of Fine Arts, Boston, MA; Gift of Mrs. Maxim Karolik for the Karolik Collection of American Paintings, 1815-1865.

Cat. #60: Hugo Gerhard Simberg, *Death on Skates*, c. 1917, etching, 4¹⁵⁄₁₆″ h. x 7³⁄₁₆″ w., USFSA; Gillis Grafstrom Collection.